KITCHEN
IDEAS THAT WORK

Creative design solutions for your home

BETH VEILLETTE

The Taunton Press

The Taunton Press
Inspiration for hands-on living®

The Taunton Press, Inc.,
63 South Main Street, PO Box 5506,
Newtown, CT 06470-5506
e-mail: tp@taunton.com

Editors: Josh Garskof and Jennifer Matlack
Jacket/Cover design: Douglas Riccardi/Memo
Interior design: Carol Petro
Layout: Lissi Sigillo and Carol Petro
Illustrator: Christine Erikson
Front cover photos: (top row, left to right) © Rob Karosis; © Mark Samu/Samu Studios; © Adrianne DePolo; © Ken Gutmaker; (middle row, left to right) © Eric Roth; © Randy O'Rourke; (bottom row, left to right) © Mark Samu/Samu Studios; © Brian Vanden Brink, Photographer 2006; (far right) © Paul Bardagjy.
Back cover photos: (clockwise from top left) © Rob Karosis; © Rob Karosis; © Matt Millman; © Roger Turk/Northlight Photographer; © Brian Vanden Brink, Photographer 2006; © Eric Roth; © Anne Gummerson.

Library of Congress Cataloging-in-Publication Data
Veillette, Beth.
  Kitchen ideas that work / Beth Veillette.
     p. cm.
  Includes bibliographical references and index.
  ISBN-13: 978-1-56158-837-4 (alk. paper)
  ISBN-10: 1-56158-837-7 (alk. paper)
  1. Kitchens–Remodeling. I. Title.

TH4816.3.K58V45 2007
747.7'97–dc22
                                                                    2006017986

Printed in the United States of America
10 9 8 7 6

ACKNOWLEDGMENTS

Writing this book has been an incredible journey. I owe a great deal of gratitude to many people for their contributions in the making of this book.

First, I am proud to be associated with The Taunton Press. I would especially like to thank my senior editor, Carolyn Mandarano, for giving me the opportunity to author this book, and especially for her guidance and support throughout this project. I had the pleasure of working with two of the best editors in the business, Jennifer Matlack and Josh Garskof, who were both efficient task masters and always managed to push me hard enough to produce my best. Thank you both for your motivation and hard work.

While writing this book, I have met many talented photographers and designers. I thank all of you for your major contributions.

I would also like to thank the very special and talented people I work with every day. Steve Hanford introduced me to his world of kitchen design and fabrication 13 years ago and has been a friend, mentor, and constant supporter ever since. To the rest of my dream team: Rob Sharp, Phil Senical, Eric Eldridge, Marc Bezanson, and Bob Berry, thank you each for the quality of your craftsmanship and your participation in implementing my kitchen designs, carrying out every last detail to perfection. To the Kountry Kraft team I deal with daily—Tom Tice, Andy Little, and Brian Tice—thank you for the safety net. To Linda Beamesdorfer, Dave Heffley, Joan Strickler, John Strickler, Scott Martin, Scott Peters, Dale Walmer, Hank Riley, and Rick Baumann, thank you for your professionalism, efficiency, and impeccable quality standards in your collective role as cabinetmakers producing work that exceed expectations.

I would especially like to thank my family. To my loving parents, Norma and Bill Meyers. I thank you Dad for always encouraging me to take risks and to embrace challenge, and Mom, for your boundless enthusiasm and support for every venture I have undertaken. My siblings have been invaluable supporters, cheering me on every step of the way. Thank you for understanding when I couldn't attend family functions or arrived late without the customary potluck dish.

To my loving husband, Pat, who covered for me in so many ways ensuring that I always had the time I needed to write. And to my sons, Patrick and Michael, both college students who are constant inspirations through their work ethic and determination to always get the paper written, even if it meant pulling an all-nighter. Thank you for all your love and encouragement, even when I couldn't do your laundry for you. And a special thanks to Patrick, who assisted me with research and data compilation when I was pressed for time.

CONTENTS

INTRODUCTION

Today's kitchen isn't so different from what it was when I was a kid. It's where I did my homework, baked cookies with Mom, colored Easter eggs, and carved pumpkins as a family. As an adult, one of my most cherished memories is making lobster bisque with my mom in my kitchen. I don't remember the bisque as much as I remember just about every moment of the time we spent working and socializing together that afternoon.

With today's typical family running in different directions, family members can find comfort and relaxation as they join together in the kitchen.

Because of the availability of incredible-looking appliances, phenomenal cabinetry styles and finishes, and beautiful countertop materials, we no longer need to keep the kitchen out of sight. Today's social kitchen is often open to a family room and/or includes a lounge area—a table and chairs, a breakfast bar, or a table with banquettes. Guests and family members are invited to join in and are comfortable as spectators sipping a cup of coffee on a counter stool or jumping in and helping out with meal prep. A new kitchen won't make you a better cook, but you can design it so that it makes the time you spend doing chores, preparing meals, or socializing with friends and family more rewarding and enjoyable.

Here I open up to you the world of kitchens—creative designs, successful solutions for tight spaces, new materials that add just the right touch of pizzazz and practicality. Although the photos will inspire you and help you dream about the many styles and finishes available, you'll also learn the pros and cons of different materials and types of components you will encounter as you revitalize your kitchen. My goal is to motivate you to get started on what will likely be the most important home improvement project you'll ever undertake.

PLANNING

There's a gorgeous new kitchen in your future, one that updates the feel of your entire home—and one where it's easy to cook, comfortable to eat,

YOUR

and welcoming to just hang out. Getting there will be a big job, but it doesn't have to be a nightmare, if you plan your project right.

KITCHEN

Choosing a Style

Let the style of your house be a guide when you're planning the overall look of your kitchen. A Craftsman bungalow, for example, might lend itself to natural cherry or quartersawn oak cabinets with flat-panel doors. A home from the Victorian era might look great with white painted cabinetry and an ornate crown molding. And a contemporary house might call for sleek unpaneled doors with a band of contrasting color running through them. Of course, since most of us don't live in houses that fit neatly into any classic architectural style, you can pick and choose your design theme, as long as it's in keeping with the overall feel of the home (be it traditional or contemporary, simple or ornate). In fact, many post–World War II houses can easily be taken in nearly any stylistic direction, from retro 1920s to French country to mid-century modern. Or you can create something eclectic that borrows from multiple styles.

left · A contemporary style can be achieved with contrasting colors, modern fixtures, and stainless finishes. In this space, the natural maple cabinetry stands out against the polished black granite counters. Decorative pendant lights and the stainless-steel island top, table legs, and range hood further convey a contemporary feel.

above · This contemporary kitchen is decidedly Asian thanks to rice paper panels on the refrigerator and the doors of the wall cabinets. Driving home this Eastern influence is cabinetry in natural cherry and stone flooring in soft, muted colors.

facing page · Details make the difference. Adding interest to this space in a light palette is the decorative, wrought-iron pot rack, the treasured collectables displayed above the wall cabinets, and box beams that span the length of the ceiling. The tile floor does its part by adding a measure of pattern.

Kitchen style goes beyond crown moldings and door panel configurations, of course. You'll also need to choose everything from the countertops to the color palette, from the eating arrangement to the way the space opens onto the adjoining rooms. There are no right or wrong solutions to any of these design challenges. You simply need to make choices that appeal to you and that work well together. The information here will help guide you through all of these decisions.

above · Just because space is limited doesn't mean your kitchen has to give up style or design. Here, an appealing 8-ft.-long kitchen packs in all the necessities: two under-cabinet refrigerators, a two-burner cooktop, two sinks, plenty of cabinets, and (installed in the right upper cabinet) a small electric oven.

facing page · An island does more than provide an additional work surface. This light wood version serves as an eating, storage, and even play area—toys belonging to the owners' small children occupy one of the built-in shelves. When set on casters, like this one, islands can be fairly versatile workhorses.

Historically, tiger maple was reserved for the affluent because it's more difficult to come by than standard maple. Here, tiger maple cabinetry in a dark finish is reminiscent of the Queen Anne or Federal period. The antique stove underscores the style of the room.

Kitchen Checklist

Figuring out the new design of your kitchen requires asking the following key questions:

- What do you like and dislike about your current kitchen?
- Do you plan to start a family or have more children? If so, will the footprint of your existing kitchen need to expand?
- Will your choices of materials and appliances or the layout of your space increase or decrease the resale value of your home?
- Do you want seating? If so, do you prefer an island, a peninsula, or an area for tables and chairs?
- How much storage space do you and your family need?
- Are you drawn to natural woods or painted finishes?
- Do you want more than one oven or a larger single oven? Does oven height matter to you?
- Does your kitchen need to accommodate more than one cook?
- Does your family need a command center where you pay bills, organize schedules, and work on a computer or laptop?
- Would you like your microwave built in? Can it be in a base cabinet?
- Separate from the oven, do you want the ability to keep food warm?
- Do you have any physical limitations that might affect the placement of elements of the kitchen?

Mixing Materials Enlivens a Kitchen

To keep this kitchen light and airy and yet add a sense of elegance, the homeowners of this late-19th-century fishing camp turned private residence combined a mix of materials in contrasting hues. Soapstone counters and marble mosaic flooring lend a refined look to the space, whereas a hard maple butcher block and the pale yellow cabinetry add warmth and a casual feeling. Together, the materials' distinct characteristics and colors balance and play off one another.

Formerly a bunk-style bedroom, the room required a complete overhaul. A refurbished antique stove was installed and floor-to-ceiling cabinets were built to fit; their soft color reflects light into the space. The oiled soapstone countertops dramatically complement the stove and highlight the cabinets. Black accent tiles in the floor tie the black and yellow color scheme together. An apron sink, crown molding, and reproduction schoolhouse-style hanging pendant lamps were installed to pay further homage to the space's early beginnings.

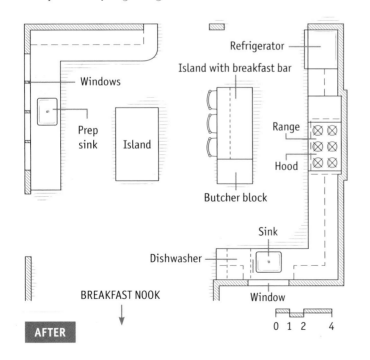

Windows

Prep sink

Island

Island with breakfast bar

Refrigerator

Range

Hood

Butcher block

Sink

Dishwasher

BREAKFAST NOOK

Window

0 1 2 4

AFTER

top · Beaded inset doors on face-frame cabinetry are used in this warm and airy kitchen. Period-style lighting fixtures, open shelving, traditional crown molding, and an apron sink all work together to convey a traditional look.

bottom · Nestled beside the center island, a 6-in.-thick maple butcher block provides functional and aesthetic charm, and can be used as a cutting board. Over time, years of marks and cuts will create a patina that adds character.

right · The designer topped the center island with dark-colored soapstone to give it visual weight, increasing its importance.

Gathering Ideas

The first step in planning your kitchen is to look at many kitchens and figure out what you like. In addition to the hundreds of spaces shown in this book, you can clip magazine and catalog photos showing features and ideas that resonate with you. You can also peruse showrooms and home centers for displays and brochures that catch your eye. Stash all of those images in a folder to show to your kitchen designer because these visuals provide the best way for him or her to begin to channel your taste and your vision into a working space.

above • Traditional white cabinetry with reproduction vintage pulls and a backsplash of pressed tin metal reflects the Victorian era of this kitchen. Despite the tight quarters, the owners made the most of the space, installing both base and wall cabinets, a deep marble countertop, and a shelf for storing everyday items.

right • In this predominately white and traditional-feeling kitchen, small details add color and visual relief, such as the green-painted island, striped rug, and warm wood floor.

Making a Wish List

Words are important too, however; and it's a good idea to create a wish list in which you can start to process exactly what features you want to include in the kitchen. Perhaps you're dreaming of professional-style appliances, a built-in restaurant-style dining booth, or glass pendant lighting. As you brainstorm about your new kitchen, jot down your thoughts. It may turn out that you won't end up with everything on your wish list, because you'll have to make compromises based on your budget, your space, or any number of other factors that arise. So, to help clarify your priorities for you and your designer from the get-go, don't make your list a simple single column of things you want. Instead, create a three-column wish list, for things you must have, things you would like to have, and things that you want if possible but could easily live without.

Create a Clip File

If you're unsure what you want in your remodel or if you have only a few vague ideas, begin identifying kitchens you find appealing. Flip through magazines devoted to the home and clip the images that catch your eye. Before you drop them into a large envelope or an accordion file, attach a sticky note on the back of each one with notations about what attracted you to that image in the first place. Was it the tile backsplash or the smart layout of the space? This exercise will help you and your kitchen designer: You'll be clearer about your renovation plans and you'll have clear examples to illustrate your vision.

Assembling Your Team

Turning your wish list into a kitchen design and then into a finished project requires assembling a team of professionals. Here are the players who might be involved:

- A *kitchen designer* is a must for any kitchen remodeling project. A good one will be extremely knowledgeable about how to arrange your floor plan and how to select appliances, countertop materials, flooring, and the like. Some designers work for home centers or cabinet shops, and their fee is included in the price that they charge for everything from appliances to cabinets to countertops. Others simply charge a flat fee, typically about 10 percent, and will work with numerous different suppliers. In either case, in addition to planning your project, the kitchen designer will also measure for, order, and install all of the kitchen components.

- A *licensed architect* is highly trained in construction design, history, and engineering. So if your job involves complex structural work or the rearranging of spaces, you'll probably want an architect (who specializes in residential renovation), in addition to the kitchen designer. Architects develop the project plans and construction drawings; for this, they typically charge either a fixed job price or an hourly rate of $100 to $200.

above • Narrow, shallow flip-up cabinets above the cooktop and counters store spices, cooking wines, and oils. Sleek and slender, the cabinets add just the right amount of style to the modest-size room without overwhelming it. They also provide a lengthy horizontal surface for displaying colorful, decorative items.

facing page • Add drama and interest to your kitchen by choosing more than one finish on your cabinetry. Here, simple white cabinetry is paired with a deep sage green ventilation hood and refrigerator cabinet, with the details delivering warmth and charm.

- A *general contractor* is the person you hire to do the main construction—from framing and wallboard installation to electrical and plumbing work. He or she may have a crew that does some of the work, but much of it will be subcontracted out to other companies. In any case, the general contractor is the buck-stops-here person who's responsible for everyone he or she hires. The general contractor's price will include all of the materials and labor and subcontractor fees for his or her part of the job, plus a markup, which is typically about 20 percent. Some kitchen designers also provide general contracting services; and some contractors, called design/builders, offer kitchen design services (look for one who has a separate design staff). And some homeowners do the general contracting themselves, which can reduce costs in exchange for a significant increase in headaches.

- On some projects, homeowners also bring in a *construction manager* to hire the general contractor and oversee the work, typically for an additional fee of 10 percent to 15 percent of the total job cost. Many architectural firms and kitchen designers offer construction management services.

right • This large island is useful for working and sitting. Lots of cabinets and drawers to store pots, pans, and other necessities and a warming drawer at the ready are on the workhorse side. Those wanting to talk to the chef or eat a meal can do so comfortably on the sitting side, thanks to the large overhang of the countertop.

facing page • Design your kitchen with the needs of your family in mind. Here, a microwave oven is placed at counter height, allowing children to reach it with ease. Snacks and cups stored on the lower shelves in the wall cabinets are equally accessible.

Design for the Ages

Consider the future needs of your family when planning your new kitchen. For example, in 10 years will your house be full of small children, teenagers, or your aged parents? Or will you have an empty nest? A few things to think about include the number, location, and height of major appliances, how much storage space you need, and whether you have counters at a variety of heights. Finally, give some thought to the overall layout of your room, keeping in mind the changing needs of each member of your family.

Transformed Space within the Same Footprint

Natural light was plentiful in this kitchen, but it didn't make up for the rustic pine cabinetry and old brick vinyl floor. The home-owners didn't need to change the footprint to create a spacious, bright new kitchen; in fact, only one doorway was moved to open up the kitchen to the family room and breakfast area.

White frameless cabinetry with full overlay Shaker-style doors and brushed nickel knobs are simple and fresh. Green granite countertops are complemented by natural maple butcher block in strategic locations, such as near the 30-in. professional-style cooktop, which is vented by a 36-in. stainless-steel hood. The natural limestone tile backsplash adds texture.

To help the family marry conversation and cooking, a kitchen table abuts the island. This design actually saved space because the aisle that would have been between two individual pieces was eliminated. When company drops by, they pull the table out to make room for another chair or two.

BEFORE

right • When you don't have enough space for both an island and a table and chairs, combine them. A custom table adjoins the work island, creating a modest eat-in kitchen.

facing page • Walls and cabinets in a crisp white and recessed downlights brighten up this space. Pairing light-colored cabinetry with reflective materials such as stainless steel or polished granite will achieve a brilliant, light-filled kitchen even when natural light is at a minimum.

— backsplash big tile ex
— several tile together?!

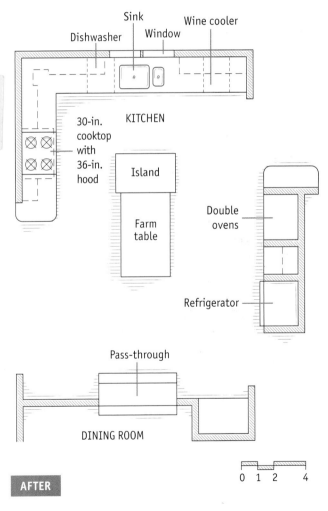

Dishwasher Sink Window Wine cooler

KITCHEN

30-in. cooktop with 36-in. hood

Island

Farm table

Double ovens

Refrigerator

Pass-through

DINING ROOM

0 1 2   4

AFTER

A Pull-Out Computer Counter

If you like the idea of having a workstation in your kitchen but don't have the space or budget for one, consider an alternative solution. This clever pull-out shelf, made to accommodate a laptop and a mouse, provides an instant work surface. Affordable and compact, it lets the homeowner refer to downloaded recipes or order groceries online. And the best part: It slides back into the base cabinetry, keeping the computer out of sight until it's needed again.

The best place to find any of these professionals is by personal reference. Talk to friends and neighbors who have recently undergone similar projects. Ask to see their projects. Ask them to tell you the highs and lows of working with their team, and find out if they would hire the same people again. Collect referrals for both designers and contractors, because once you choose one of them, he or she can likely recommend people to consider for the other members of the team. Once you have a handful of referrals, ask them to come and look at your job and give you an estimate. Try to get three itemized bids in hand, and then make your hire based not on the bottom line but on how good the referrals were, on your impressions of the professionals' personalities, and on your gut instinct. (Do avoid anyone who bids much lower or much higher than the pack, however, because that's very likely an indicator of trouble to come during the project.) And try not to let impatience to get the job done affect who you hire. It's better to wait for quality than to get an inferior job done quickly.

above • To help maintain a good traffic flow to the screened porch and patio just outside this kitchen, the food prep areas were tucked into a corner.

left • Even if you're on a very tight budget you can have fun with materials and color. These plywood cabinets are decorated with medium-density fiberboard panels. The industrial feel is enhanced by the concrete floors and cantilevered shelves.

facing page • Typical of apartments in which space is at a real premium, this one features a contemporary, albeit narrow, kitchen. A mix of materials and colors highlight the eclectic feel.

Crunching the Budget

How do you mesh your wish list with your budget to figure out what you can afford? You can try to ballpark the numbers by talking to retailers, but there's only one reliable way to put a number on your job. You need to get prices from kitchen designers and general contractors. And the only way to get accurate numbers from them is to pinpoint all of the details you want for your project so that they can price them accordingly.

Picking out such specifics as the actual countertop stone, the line of cabinets, and the model numbers for your appliances will get you the most accurate project prices. (A professional designer—and some contractors—can help you with this process, from both design and financial points of view.) There may be some decisions that you need to leave until later, but the more that's left undecided, the greater the chances that your project will run over budget because the contractor or designer was not able to plan enough money in the bid to cover what you end up selecting.

It's also a good idea to set aside at least 10 percent of your budget as a contingency fund. Try to complete your project without that money, so it will be there when something unforeseen inevitably comes up late in the game.

right • **A TV is now a staple in many kitchens. This one, mounted in an upper cabinet unit, is kept off precious countertop space and is visible from most areas of the room.**

Connecting Kitchen to Den

Having made the decision to renovate their kitchen, the homeowners of this 70-sq.-ft. kitchen were faced with the challenge of how to make it feel larger and more inviting. Adding on wasn't an option, but removing a wall was.

A den, accessible only through the dining room, also got transformed because the wall separating it from the kitchen was removed. This allowed a counter area and breakfast table to be installed, creating much needed gathering space for the homeowners' growing family. Contemporary furniture for the new eating area further connects the space to the flush frameless maple cabinetry in the kitchen.

The kitchen also gained natural light and a view from the three windows in the den. Glass doors on the wall cabinets and polished granite countertops do their part to add spaciousness to the room by reflecting the natural light.

left • By removing the wall that separated the small den and even smaller kitchen area, the homeowners transformed each room into bright, inviting spaces. The kitchen, once dark and drab, now benefits from the natural light pouring in from the den windows.

BEFORE

A LAYOUT

What shape will your countertop follow? Where will the appliances go?

Making smart layout decisions requires understanding

a few rules of thumb about how kitchens work.

THAT

Whatever the size of your room, your budget, and your wish list,

the secret of kitchen success lies in how you put the pieces together.

WORKS

Kitchen Shape

The first step in designing your new kitchen is to visualize the potential of the space. It can be difficult to see past the existing configuration of cabinets and appliances, but that's exactly what you need to do. Try to imagine that you have completely gutted your old kitchen—taking it right down to the walls. Consider only the size and shape of the room as well as the location of doorways, staircases, and windows. To help open your mind to the possibilities, take a look at the common kitchen shapes shown in "The Work Triangle," on p. 34. You or your designer should create a scale drawing of the space and experiment with different arrangements of everything from cabinets to countertops to appliances to find the right layout for your new kitchen.

above • When floor tiles are placed so they run the length of the kitchen they visually elongate the space, as seen in this galley kitchen.

left • Natural details, from the window blinds to the counter stools and baskets, blend with traditional white-painted cabinets for textural effect.

facing page • This open kitchen feels slightly more grounded thanks to the crown molding at the ceiling and the wide baseboard trim around the island.

GRABBING MORE SPACE

There's one thing your new kitchen may need that you can't buy from any supply house, home center, or catalog: more space. Because you will spend so much time in the kitchen, doing everything from cooking to eating to socializing, you'll want as much square footage as possible for the room. There are a few different ways you can get it:

- *Add on:* The ultimate answer to the problem of too little space is to build an addition. That will ratchet up the costs and hassles of the job, of course, because it involves not only a lot more labor and materials but also additional types of work, such as earth moving, foundation pouring, and roofing. Still, as long as you're going through the significant expense of installing a new kitchen, this is a good time to consider wrapping an addition into your plans. Otherwise, you might find yourself re-remodeling in the near future.

- *Bump out:* In some cases, you may be able to create a small-scale addition without having to dig up the yard and pour a foundation. A bump-out literally pokes out from the side of the existing structure. This can be an economical way to gain, say, 30 sq. ft. or 40 sq. ft. of floor space, which could be the difference between having room for an eating area and not.

above • This kitchen setup provides many levels of storage—from the coffee-colored island and pantry to built-in white cabinetry—good traffic flow around work areas, and a view from the island seating to the adjoining rooms.

left • Brick and knotty pine combine to create an interesting textural effect. The details of this kitchen—from the exposed ceiling beams to the turned table legs and scrolled wrought-iron light fixture—enliven the space.

facing page • In an unusual treatment, tile continues to the ceiling of this small kitchen, making the room feel taller. If this room were larger, the bold tones of the tile might be overwhelming; but here, they add punch.

Making Good Use of a Small Space

Built in the mid-1800s as a summer house, this shingle-style home was in need of a kitchen renovation. The owners, now grandparents, wanted an up-to-date, open, and friendly space where they could relax and enjoy their family. The existing kitchen, originally built as a servant's kitchen, was a dead-end space at the back of the house. To achieve the homeowners' goal of expansion, the architect gave the kitchen a couple of small bumps rather than an extensive addition. A breakfast area was created in what was originally an outdoor terrace, and a sitting room was claimed and opened up to the kitchen space. By accessing the sitting room, the kitchen would be open to views of the backyard. The center chimney was cleverly disguised by wrapping it on all four sides with cabinetry and appliances.

The creamy white paint with glaze finish on the new cabinetry is accentuated by the dark-stained oak flooring. The glass and mullion doors on the cabinetry were carefully designed to mimic the transoms over the windows of the house. To echo the extensive use of stone in the home, granite was the natural choice for the countertops and backsplashes.

above right • A small breakfast area was added on in what was originally an outdoor terrace. The owners decided to leave the chimney intact but obscure it with cabinetry and appliances.

facing page • After removing a dividing wall, the small kitchen was opened up to the adjoining sitting room with its abundance of windows. The new design floods the new kitchen with natural light and offers an attractive view of the property.

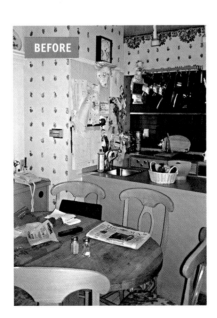

BEFORE

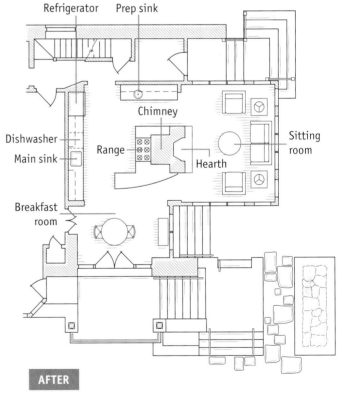

Refrigerator Prep sink

Chimney

Dishwasher

Main sink

Range

Hearth

Sitting room

Breakfast room

AFTER

- *Take from other room(s)*: Sometimes you can add space to the kitchen without building an addition at all. You can annex existing square footage from an adjacent dining room, closet, breezeway, porch, garage, or utility room to get the square footage you need. To take advantage of the space, you'll have to remove or relocate walls, which requires the expertise of an architect or contractor, who will know whether beams or other structural supports must be installed. The closet, laundry room, bathroom, pantry, or porch may be eliminated, relocated, or resized to give you the extra room you need.

- *Reconfigure the existing space*: Or you can simply better use the kitchen's existing square footage. In many older houses, for example, all of the counters and appliances were installed in an L along two adjoining walls, leaving the other half of the room open for a table and chairs. Just by taking over all four walls for your new cabinets, countertops and appliances, you're in essence doubling the size of your kitchen while keeping it within the original footprint. And if you include a breakfast bar on an island or peninsula in the middle of the room, you won't miss that dinette set at all.

- *Open the floor plan*: Another option is to remove one or more of the kitchen walls, opening up the space to an adjacent dining or family room. Put a large island where the wall had been and you'll wind up with a kitchen that feels much bigger than it is. Even simply relocating picture windows and sliding glass doors can make room for new banks of pantry cabinets; and removing interior doors from their openings can make the kitchen feel more spacious.

top • An extra-large bay window provides lots of natural light and beautiful views. The oversize island features drawers and shelves on multiple sides to ensure adequate storage.

bottom • This beverage center located just outside the kitchen proper becomes an auxiliary workspace when entertaining. It features a wet bar sink, an ice maker and refrigerator, a wine rack, and cabinetry for storing stemware.

An Island on Wheels

Having lived in their nondescript 1950s ranch for nearly 7 years, the homeowners decided they were ready for a change. The kitchen was small and uninviting, with a cramped eat-in area. To transform the space into the room they always imagined—open, airy, and bright—a major overhaul was necessary. The project's design team removed a few walls and relocated a stairwell, which gave them a large open space in which to work. French doors and larger windows were installed to bring natural light into the area.

The homeowners wanted a place in the kitchen where their two young children could work on arts and crafts projects. The architect designed an island with open shelves for storing supplies. Even though there was plenty of room for the island, the owners were concerned that it might be in the way when they entertained and needed to expand the dining room table to seat their extended family. The architect came up with a clever solution: He outfitted the island with rolling casters that lock into place for stability. This allowed the island to be moved out of the center of the kitchen and dock in a more favorable location. To facilitate the docking of the island, the architect designed a notch in the island counter that fit into a nearby wall-hugging countertop.

The new flooring used throughout the renovation is bamboo, which is durable, harder, and more environmentally friendly than many hardwoods commonly used for flooring. The natural maple, flush, full-overlay frameless cabinetry and polished synthetic stone countertops give the kitchen its contemporary appeal.

left · Arts and crafts supplies for the young budding artists of the family are stored neatly in easy-to-reach, open shelves below the countertop. The opposite end of the island is used as kitchen work space and is outfitted with storage for cooking utensils.

right · During the holidays when extra space is needed for the expanded dining table, the island moves out of the center of the room and parks itself neatly against a permanent countertop. A notch in the island top allows the unit to fit perfectly.

The Work Zones

When you think about it, every kitchen consists of many separate work areas. There's the place where you do your chopping and have your knives and cutting boards nearby, for example, and a cleanup station consisting of the sink, dishwasher, and trash receptacle. Even the spot where you stage groceries before loading them into the refrigerator is an important work area. The secret to designing a great kitchen is to think about all of the work zones you'll need, what each one requires to be efficient, and how they should work together.

For starters, that means creating a work triangle. When you're cooking, you use three components of your kitchen more than any others—the refrigerator, range (or cooktop), and sink. So designers usually try to keep these essentials out of the major traffic flow, to put them relatively close together, and to locate each one at the point of an imaginary triangle. The work triangle isn't the only way to go, but it does offer the easiest access to these three essential kitchen tools with the least walking to and fro. Ideally, the three legs of the triangle should add up to 26 ft. or less—with each individual leg measuring between 4 ft. and 9 ft. Once you've plotted out your work triangle, you can begin to design each of the individual work zones.

The Work Triangle

Your kitchen layout will be determined by two factors: the size and shape of your space and the placement of work areas within the room based on the work triangle, an imaginary line drawn to connect the refrigerator, sink, and cooktop or range. Ideally, each leg of the work triangle should be between 4 ft. and 9 ft. long. Islands and peninsulas should not intersect the triangle by more than 12 in.

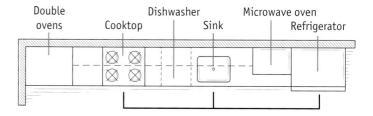

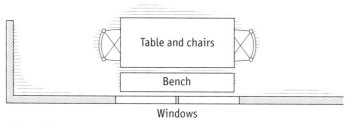

Single wall

Although not really a triangle, this layout works well because there is ample counter space between each appliance, 24 in. or more. Separate wall ovens do not need to be within the work triangle because they are not typically used as often as the sink, refrigerator, and cooktop. The opposite wall can be a great place for a table and chairs. A table also can double as a work surface when necessary.

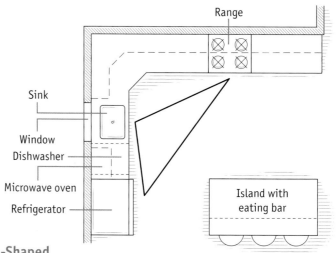

L-Shaped

The L-shaped kitchen is an ideal arrangement for an island, especially when the kitchen is open to the family room because it connects the spaces together.

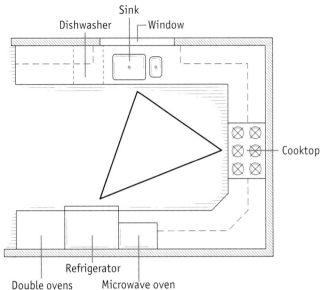

Labels: Dishwasher, Sink, Window, Cooktop, Refrigerator, Double ovens, Microwave oven

U-Shaped

The U-shaped kitchen is considered by many to be the most efficient layout. The legs of the triangle are nearly equal in length, allowing ample counter space between each appliance yet not too many steps between work zones.

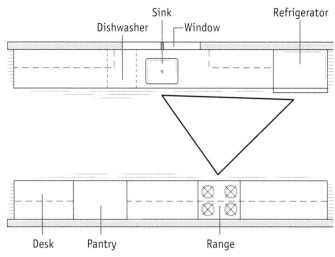

Labels: Dishwasher, Sink, Window, Refrigerator, Desk, Pantry, Range

Galley

By positioning appliances on both walls of a galley kitchen, you can establish a good work triangle. The main drawback to a galley layout is that traffic can get congested within work zones. Maintaining an aisle of 4 ft. to 5 ft. will lessen traffic congestion.

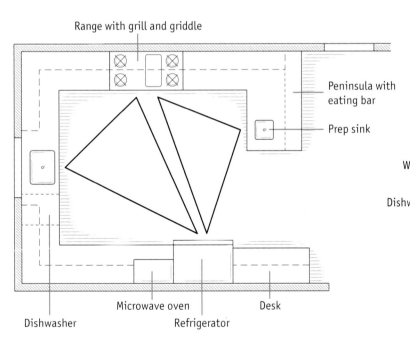

Labels: Range with grill and griddle, Peninsula with eating bar, Prep sink, Dishwasher, Microwave oven, Refrigerator, Desk

G-Shaped

The G-shaped kitchen is an ideal arrangement for two cooks because there is ample room for two people to share in the cooking and cleaning duties simultaneously. Including a prep sink produces two work triangles. Kitchen desks are best located at the end of a run of cabinetry; otherwise, the refrigerator or a tall pantry cabinet, both large anchors, are good ways to end the run.

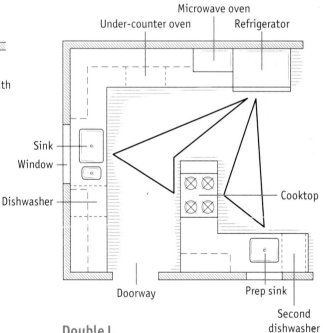

Labels: Microwave oven, Under-counter oven, Refrigerator, Sink, Window, Dishwasher, Cooktop, Doorway, Prep sink, Second dishwasher

Double L

Two separate work triangles are present for multiple cooks. By positioning the cooktop in a peninsula, cooks can use it from either side.

CLEANUP

The primary kitchen sink needs to be in a central spot and should get at least 24 in. of countertop on one side and 18 in. on the other. Place the dishwasher within 36 in. of the sink (to the left if you're right handed or vice versa). And think about a trash and recycling station on the sink's opposite flank. Because the sink is where you'll spend the most time working in the kitchen—and because cleanup gets boring—it's nice to locate a large window above the sink. A small flat-screen television can also be installed nearby.

FOOD STORAGE

Try to keep the refrigerator close to the doorway where you'll be carting in groceries from the car. You'll want at least 15 in. of countertop on the handle side of the fridge—or within arm's length of it—for staging foodstuffs. And the same rules apply for large pantry cabinets, even though they aren't part of the work triangle itself.

above • This kitchen fits perfectly with the casual lifestyle of the homeowners. Floor tile is easy to keep clean but can be hard on your back if you're standing on it for long periods of time.

left • An expanded, arched doorway sets off the kitchen from the rest of the house. A farm table can double as extra seating or a place to prep meals.

facing page • A six-burner stove needs good ventilation, provided for in this glass and steel hood. Lights in the hood provide welcome illumination when cooking on the stovetop.

Annexing an Adjacent Room

The homeowners of this cottage-style home wanted a country look for their new kitchen that would appear as though it were original to the house. Space was at a premium and adding on was not an option.

To increase the size of the kitchen without building an addition, the designer annexed an adjoining bathroom. (The bathroom was relocated to another part of the house.) More space was allotted to the kitchen by moving the back door a few feet and eliminating another door. Raising the height of a window allowed for a longer counter run.

A 30-in.-wide built-in refrigerator was chosen, along with a 30-in. professional-style range. The homeowners used barn red, beaded-inset, flat-panel doors for the cabinetry and granite countertops. The homeowners also found reclaimed wormy chestnut flooring, and the cabinetmakers fabricated a wormy chestnut faux post, which is actually a pipe chase concealing the plumbing pipes to the second floor.

An interesting aspect of this kitchen is the swinging window. Reluctant to replace the original wavy glass, the homeowner modified the old window, making it shorter, and fashioned a hinge-and-hook system to support the new window when it is open.

right • A gas range and a built-in refrigerator–freezer leave just enough room for an 18-in.-wide pantry. Salvaged 100-year-old wormy chestnut replaced the original fir flooring, which was deemed beyond repair.

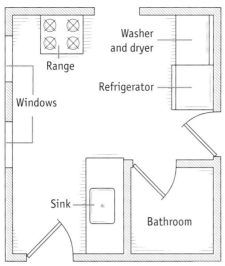

Washer
and dryer

Range

Refrigerator

Windows

Sink

Bathroom

BEFORE

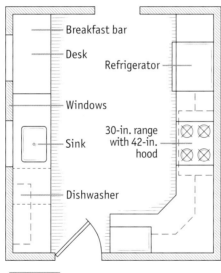

Breakfast bar

Desk

Refrigerator

Windows

Sink

30-in. range
with 42-in.
hood

Dishwasher

AFTER

top right · Cabinets with chicken-wire doors are as useful as they are decorative. The pot filler is a favorite fixture of the homeowners and saves them from lugging big stockpots full of water across the kitchen from the sink.

bottom right · Rather than give up an antique glass pane that was original to the house, the homeowner reconfigured the old window to a barn sash style for use in the new, shorter opening. A hook in the ceiling supports the unit, letting in the breeze.

COOKING

If you're using a vintage or professional range, you're probably going to make it the focal point of the kitchen, putting it in the middle of the most visible wall. But even if you're choosing a more modest-looking range (or cooktop), it should be centrally located. Plan at least 15 in. of countertop on one side of the range and 9 in. on the other. A pullout drawer or hanging rack for storing pots and pans should be nearby. And locate frequently used utensils and pot holders within reach. Wall ovens and microwaves need not be part of the work triangle, but they do need at least 15 in. of counter space next to them. A microwave can be mounted in a base cabinet, but placing it higher (ideally, with its bottom 48 in. off the floor) will be a lot more convenient.

FOOD PREP

You'll also want to create a space specifically designed for the hands-on jobs of cooking, from chopping vegetables to kneading dough to mixing batter. For this you'll want a 36-in.-wide stretch of dedicated countertop. If you're using anything less than the toughest countertop material for your kitchen, think about a more durable material here. And if you're significantly taller or shorter than the average person, you might consider something other than the standard 36-in. countertop height for the prep center (although this might be seen as a draw-back to a potential homebuyer someday). Think about locating appliance garages in the area, and if it's far from the primary sink, about putting a small additional sink with a garbage disposal here. If two cooks often work at the same time in your kitchen, try to incorporate two prep centers.

far left · Supported by an X fashioned out of steel and bolted to the peninsula cabinetry, this clever glass table makes the most of limited space for casual dining.

left · Storage is a must in any kitchen, regardless of its size. Pullout wooden shelves allow the contents of the base cabinets to be completely viewed, making these deep cabinets as practical as possible.

A Hide-Away Cutting Board

With all the chopping and slicing that goes on in the kitchen, cutting boards are a necessity. Options include butcher-block-topped islands, individual wood or plastic cutting boards that can be stored away in base cabinets after use, or slide-out boards such as this one. When food prep is through, the thick block simply slides back into the island until it's needed

SERVING

Create a spot that's out of the cook's way where you can set out buffet-style meals, crudités, and hors d'oeuvres. Ideally, your serving area will be located where the kitchen intersects adjacent living spaces. If possible, locate storage cabinets for serving dishes at arm's reach. A warming oven is another handy feature to place nearby. You might also raise the countertop to 42 in., which is not only convenient for serving but also for pulling up a stool and eating because serving areas often double as breakfast bars.

WET BAR

Whether installed in a kitchen, dining room, or family room, a wet bar is an extension of the kitchen. In addition to a few feet of countertop, you'll want plenty of cabinets designed for holding liquor and glassware, a small sink, a refrigerator with an ice maker, and possibly a wine cooler. Another popular option is to install an additional dishwasher in the wet bar.

above • Concrete and butcher block combine to accommodate multiple chefs. Open shelves below the countertop provide ready access to bowls and dishes.

left • A butler's pantry connects the kitchen to the formal dining room. Often, second cleanup sinks and dishwashers are located in these spaces, which are put to good use during large-scale entertaining.

facing page • Wall cabinets installed above the end of this counter provide a compact space for a microwave and a cabinet for storing coffee mugs and teacups. An espresso machine sits just beneath the microwave oven, making this area an efficient gourmet snack center.

DESK AREA

Kitchens also often serve as de facto home offices. Here's where you may do everything from paying monthly bills to writing Christmas cards to making tedious customer service calls. And thanks to the ever-shrinking size of office equipment, putting a fully functioning home office in the kitchen requires surprisingly little room. All you need is 3 ft. to 4 ft. of wall space that's segregated from your cooking and eating zones. A countertop makes an ideal desktop when installed at 30 in. off the floor with a 24-in.- to 30-in.-wide knee space underneath. (If you're also installing a breakfast bar, the desk area can be at the same height, so you can share stools and eliminate the need for a desk chair.) Appliance garages or pocket doors can be used to hide computers, printers, faxes, and phones; base cabinets can serve as filing cabinets and supply drawers; and wall cabinets can offer storage for books and other necessities.

top • A bulletin board, used to tack family photos, reminders, and schedules, divides the base and upper cabinets of this command center. A center shelf provides a surface for displaying teapots and other treasured collectibles.

bottom • Cabinet doors open and slide back to reveal a TV at the end of this breakfast bar. Tucked below is a mail center. When visitors arrive, the doors close to keep clutter hidden from view.

left • A small kitchen TV, space for incoming and outgoing mail, file drawers, and a planning desk make up command central for this busy household.

Converting a Pantry into Command Central

During the planning stages of a new dream home, the homeowner insisted on a space where she could manage the household finances, access the Internet, and file away important papers. By using the space that would otherwise have been a walk-in pantry, the architect designed a home office just off the kitchen, complete with pocket doors for privacy when needed.

A U-shaped wood countertop sits on built-in storage cabinets and file drawers on two sides. The main seating area of the desk, below a window with a great view, holds a computer and keyboard. Open cabinets on the walls hold cookbooks, and a bulletin board keeps appointment cards and activity schedules. The cherry cabinetry in the office is also used in the kitchen to help link the spaces together. An added bonus is the natural light that flows from the office to the kitchen through the transom-topped glass door.

left • French pocket doors let light through but close off the office space for privacy and to keep some of the potential clutter out of sight.

below • Matching cabinetry in the office and the kitchen connect the two spaces visually. Natural light from the windows in the office illuminate the otherwise dark corner of the kitchen.

LAUNDRY

If your washer and dryer are in the basement, moving them into the kitchen is a great way to simplify a significant household chore. (Master and first-floor bathrooms are other alternatives.) A standard washer and dryer installed side by side measure about 60 in. wide and 3 ft. deep. Because they're top loading, typical washers cannot be installed under countertops and because the machines stand 42 in. or 43 in. high, they won't fit under a standard-height counter anyway. Today's ultra-efficient front-loading washers and their companion dryers, on the other hand, will fit under a 36-in.-high countertop and together some are only 50 in. wide and 26 in. deep, so they make a good choice for kitchen laundry stations. Alternatively, you can choose a stackable unit, which puts the dryer directly above the washer and so takes up only half of the floor space; laundry capacity is typically smaller, but that still beats marching up and down the basement stairs. You'll also want to plan nearby cabinets for storing laundry supplies, at least 36 in. of countertop, and perhaps a built-in ironing board that folds down from the wall. Put the whole laundry center in a closet behind pocket doors and it'll disappear when it's not in use.

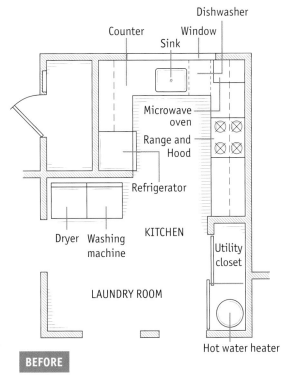

Dishwasher
Counter
Window
Sink
Microwave oven
Range and Hood
Refrigerator

KITCHEN

Dryer Washing machine

Utility closet

LAUNDRY ROOM

Hot water heater

BEFORE

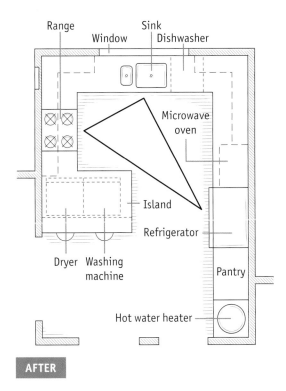

Range
Window
Sink
Dishwasher

Microwave oven

Island

Refrigerator

Dryer Washing machine

Pantry

Hot water heater

AFTER

Hiding the Laundry

During the renovation of a 1960 ranch house in Louisiana, the original laundry room was annexed into the very small kitchen so the homeowner could have more cooking space. This left the problem of where to put the washer and dryer. By replacing the existing laundry equipment with a compact front-loading washer and companion dryer, the designer was able to place the pair under the counter and behind cabinet doors at the breakfast bar. The appliances are easily accessible on wash day and hidden from view at all other times. An added feature—the large countertop becomes a folding station when the laundry is dry.

above • A peninsula with a few counter stools was more than the homeowner hoped for when she commissioned a design to make her new kitchen more open and inviting for entertaining.

left • On wash day, cabinetry reveals built-in laundry equipment. To keep things quiet, the doors are closed while the machines are operating.

Eating Areas

There's one other essential work zone for the modern kitchen, a place to eat. Even if you have a separate dining room, you'll want a spot in the kitchen where the family can enjoy casual meals, watch the chef without getting in his or her way, sit down for certain cooking tasks, and even do homework and other everyday projects. In fact, some families who are short on space decide to do away with their dining rooms (which are rarely used except for special occasions anyway) in favor of spacious eat-in kitchens and family rooms. Or they simply knock down the wall separating kitchen and dining room to link the two spaces. For your kitchen, the style of eating area you choose will have a major effect on how much square footage it requires.

TABLE AND CHAIRS

A table and chairs is the most formal choice and the best substitute for a true dining room if you don't have one. But it also requires the most floor space in the kitchen. Round tables are the most efficient, especially those with a central pedestal instead of four legs, which can get in the way of diners' knees. A 3-ft.-dia. table can accommodate four adults; a 4-ft. table can handle six. For a rectangular table, figure a 24-in.- to 30-in.-wide stretch of tabletop per person, so a 3-ft. by 4-ft. table can accommodate two diners on each side. You'll also need enough space so people can be seated a comfortable distance from the table and still allow room for others to walk around them; figure at least 36 in. between the table and the nearest wall or object, and 48 in. on the side from where you'll serve food.

top · Windows help define the eating area in this kitchen. The two main color tones in the kitchen—black and natural wood—complement the expanse of nature visible through the windows.

bottom · A built-in banquette provides the added bonus of storage drawers underneath, perfect for table linens or coloring books and crayons for the kids. The plush cushions make mealtime extra enjoyable.

facing page · This open plan provides long uninterrupted views that make the house seem larger than it is. Beams help delineate the different living areas.

BOOTH

There are good reasons why diners and restaurants install booths—they're as space efficient as they are comfy and casual. Because the benches don't move, there's no need to make room for seats to slide back from the table. And because they're pushed against corners, alcoves, or bay windows, you need not make space for people to walk around them. Plus, with drawers or hinged lids, the benches can double as storage compartments. You'll want your benches about 18 in. deep, and plan for about 24 in. of table-top for each person. But the table can overhang the seating by 3 in. or 4 in., so a four-person booth can easily fit in a 6-ft. by 6-ft. space (much less than the square footage required for a table and four chairs). Best of all, a cushy upholstered booth can provide a fun, comfortable dining experience.

right • Art Deco accents mix with traditional-style elements, such as the trim on the base of the booth and the legs of the cherry-topped table. This nook is all about fun, from the candy apple red upholstery to the pendant lights and artwork on the walls.

facing page top • Taking advantage of the corner space and the spectacular view, the owners of this kitchen added a simple eating area. Because the benches abut the wall, this arrangement requires less space than a traditional table and chairs.

facing page bottom • Custom details, such as the carved wood corbels and raised panel wainscot, grace this breakfast bar in natural cherry. The layout of the island emphasizes the kitchen area and distinguishes it from the adjoining living room.

far right facing page • While this massive island might be too large for most kitchens, its shape can be replicated in any size. The countertop overhang gently curves to provide visual appeal and adequate knee space for seated diners.

BREAKFAST BAR

The hottest trend in kitchen seating, though, is the breakfast bar located on an island or peninsula. This is simply a countertop that overhangs the cabinet to provide knee space for seating that slides up to it. The bar can be at standard height (36 in. from the floor), table height (30 in.), or raised (42 in.). In any case, the seats of the chairs or stools should be 12 in. below the countertop height. You'll want to plan a 24-in. length of countertop for each diner and 9 in. to 14 in. of knee overhang. To seat four people, you'll need a 96-in.-long bar. Keep in mind that diners are typically lined up single file, so a bar doesn't provide the same social experience as sitting across from each other at a table. Still, it's nice for snacks and breakfasts, as long as the seating is arranged toward the kitchen or a picture window instead of facing a blank wall. The bar can double as another kitchen work zone, such as a serving station or a second food prep area, and some large kitchens have both a breakfast bar and a table and chair set.

top • The four corner posts on this roomy island complement the prairie-style details in the rest of the room. Despite its aesthetic charm, the island—with a prep sink, wine storage, apothecary drawers, and built-in refrigerator—is a practical, hardworking addition to this handsome space.

bottom • If your renovation plans don't include space for a mudroom, design an area in the corner of your kitchen or pantry for organizing sports gear and outerwear. Here, a cabinet featuring hooks, open shelving, and pull-out baskets keeps all organized and within reach.

facing page • Installed at the end of a kitchen run, a planning desk is all that's needed to make a grocery list or write a quick note. The built-in shelves above are perfect for keeping a small library of cookbooks or household supplies at the ready.

Choosing Colors

There are no right or wrong choices when choosing color for your kitchen. In fact, this is an opportunity to express your own sense of style and to have some fun. Keep these tips in mind:

• Light colors tend to make spaces feel larger, whereas dark ones can make them feel smaller, so you might want to avoid dark hues for a small kitchen.

• "Hot" colors—the reds, oranges, and yellows of fire—create an invigorating atmosphere. "Cool" colors—the greens and blues of water—feel soothing and relaxed.

• Neutral colors—whites, beiges, tans, light browns, and natural stones—tend to blend well with any decorating scheme. So choosing neutrals for permanent elements of the kitchen, from tile to flooring to countertops, is the safest way to ensure you won't grow tired of your choices and that a potential home buyer won't be put off by your selections. Let the bold colors come from the details, such as window treatments and wall paint.

• Blending surfaces with different textures—such as rough-hewn stone and shiny stainless steel—can bring visual interest to the space, no matter what color scheme you've chosen.

• The grout patterns of tiled surfaces deliver another layer of texture to the space. Large tiles, which create fewer grout lines—tend to make spaces feel larger than small tiles. Long straight lines tend to make the tiled surface seem longer, while crossing lines tend to make it feel shorter. And installing tiles on the diagonal lends drama and size. The patterns can also virtually disappear if you color-match the grout to the tile.

CABINETS

Cabinets supply the bulk of the kitchen's storage as well

as the footprint that your countertops will follow,

so your cabinet choices, drawers, and specialized storage

options are essential for creating an organized and

efficient cooking area. Cabinets typically make up 40 percent

to 50 percent of the cost of remodeling a kitchen.

Face Frame or Frameless?

With this in mind, you'll want to make the selection of cabinets one of the first steps in the kitchen-planning process. While there are countless style choices for cabinets, they all fall into one of two broad categories, those with a face frame and those without.

FACE FRAME

The traditional way to build cabinets—which remains the standard for most manufacturers in the United States—is to cover the front of each cabinet with a frame of wood, typically made from strips that are about 1½ in. wide. That masks the raw edges of the cabinet box, which is typically made from plywood, medium-density fiberboard (MDF), or particleboard. And it means that oversize frame pieces (or additional lengths of frame material) can be used to cover open spaces between two cabinets or between a cabinet and a wall or appliance.

above • Knotty pine beaded inset cabinetry paired with a center island in an ebony finish create a rich, warm feeling in this space. The white marble top on the island contrasts handsomely with the cabinetry's dark granite countertops. Increasing the appeal of the space is the shapely black wrought-iron chandelier and the arched doorway.

left • To create a modern feel, the homeowners selected full-overlay, flush doors in cherry; the toasty hue of the wood adds warmth to the stainless-steel appliances and white granite countertops. Brushed-nickel hardware in a towel-bar style help tie the cabinetry and appliances together.

facing page • Storage can be beautiful. The glass doors on this tall cabinet show off a wide assortment of pitchers, bowls, and platters. Beside it, rows of square shelves create a handsome unit for storing wine and other bottled beverages.

IVORINE

FOR WASHING

A face frame can also mimic the built-in look of the classic cabinetry found in old houses. Combined with inset doors, which sit completely inside the opening so they're flush with the face when closed, a face frame can provide an authentic replica of historic cabinetry. But a face frame cabinet doesn't necessarily have to wear inset doors or look old-fashioned. You can use full-overlay doors, which cover nearly the entire face frame, or partial-overlay doors, which sit over part of the face frame and are less costly to build and install than either inset or full-overlay doors. Any of these doors can be outfitted with either traditional detailing, such as a raised, flat, or bead-board panel, or modern styling, such as unadorned flush veneer plywood.

No matter what style of door you choose, remember that the face frame covers a bit of the cabinet opening. This reduces the clearance for getting large items in and out of storage. It also means that drawers and other pullouts have to be sized to fit inside the face frame, making them slightly smaller than they would be in frameless cabinetry.

top left · Full-overlay doors convey a clean, simple look in this warm, sun-filled kitchen. Wide as the cabinets themselves and totally concealing the cabinets' frames, full-overlay doors are available in a range of styles from Shaker to modern.

top right · These painted cabinets embody the Shaker style with their color, leaded-glass doors, and simplicity. A soapstone counter and sink complete the look.

left · For homeowners who enjoy cooking and entertaining, this kitchen, which is open to the family room, is perfect. A half-circle eating bar can be lowered when not in use, and a wood buffet counter provides additional storage underneath.

facing page · Open shelving units designed into a center island provide a handy storage solution. In addition, these uniform cubbies filled with a mix of dishware in various shades offer a delightful way to add color and texture to a room.

True Full-Overlay Doors

Full-overlay doors are often chosen for the tidy, simplified look they impart on frameless and face-frame cabinetry. The doors are mounted so that they completely cover the frame of the cabinet, including any hinges. To make certain you're getting what you've paid for, take a close look at your cabinetry. Large and inconsistent gaps (sometimes up to 1 in.) between the doors and the drawer heads results in an uneven, disorderly look. Good-quality cabinetry with full-overlay doors should leave a consistent 1/8 in. of space between the doors and the drawers, giving a tidy, flush appearance.

FRAMELESS

Created in post–World War II Europe, frameless (or European) cabinets replace the traditional decorative face frame with a thin tape-like strip of wood or other finish material laid onto the edges of the box. That cuts manufacturing costs and makes for larger cabinet openings, which maximizes drawer sizes and accessibility to whatever is stowed inside. And installers can still use extra finish material as fillers to hide spaces between cabinets and alongside appliances and walls.

Stylistically, frameless cabinets that are combined with flush (nonpaneled) overlay doors can make for a very modern look. Or you can get all of the convenience of a frameless cabinet without the ultra-modern effect by selecting a classic paneled door and the appropriate knobs and pulls. Whatever style of door you choose, however, using frameless cabinetry requires full-overlay doors. So, although they can convey a vintage style, these cabinets will never offer the totally authentic traditional appearance of inset doors.

above • Although they are fairly compact, microwave ovens are often one of the most difficult appliances to locate in the kitchen. This microwave, installed at a comfortable level, steals a small amount of space in a tall, freestanding storage cabinet. Below it, deep wide drawers provide ample storage, while the cabinet above keeps cookbooks in order.

left • You can't go wrong with white cabinets. They are versatile enough to be paired with everything from black to more white, as in this kitchen. The stainless-steel tile backsplash and cabinet hardware add a touch of contemporary flair.

facing page • These cabinets make space for a microwave that's accessible to children.

Cabinetry

The first thing you'll learn when you begin shopping for kitchen cabinetry is that there are three categories of cabinets to choose from: stock, semicustom, and custom. Don't assume that these terms indicate a level of quality. Within each group, there exists a low and a high end. How should you decide which type is best for you? Choose the highest quality cabinet you can comfortably afford.

CUSTOM

STOCK
$

- Readily available; usually ships 1 week to 3 weeks after order is placed.
- Homeowner can install.
- Limited selections of sizes, styles, wood species, finishes, and storage accessories.
- Cost-cutting construction methods and materials used.
- Available in only standard sizes so may require filler pieces to cover gaps.

SEMICUSTOM
$$

- Offers greater design flexibility than stock.
- Decent range of styles, sizes, materials, finishes, and built-in storage options.
- Some customization available on heights and depths.
- Available 6 weeks to 8 weeks after order is placed.
- Like stock, may require filler strips to cover gaps.

CUSTOM
$$$

- Unlimited variety of sizes, shapes, styles, wood species, and finishes.
- Can be elaborately designed and embellished with architectural features.
- Limitless built-in options.
- Can cost 25 percent more than semicustom cabinets.
- Available 8 weeks to 16 weeks after order is placed.

SEMICUSTOM

STOCK

Custom cabinetry allows your kitchen to reflect your personal style. Here, black distressed maple cabinetry coupled with cherry creates an individualized space. In addition, a mix of countertop materials—butcher block and granite— underscores the distinctiveness of the room.

Custom, Stock, or In-Between

Many factors affect the price of cabinets—from the style of the doors and drawer fronts to the choice of materials, finish, and hardware. But more than anything, the cost of cabinets is determined by whether you have them made to order, buy them "off the rack," or choose the middle ground.

CUSTOM

When a cabinetmaker or carpenter custom-builds your cabinets to order, there's no limit to what you can get. Want your doors and drawer fronts made from mahogany, cherry, or recycled antique barn wood? No problem. Or perhaps everyone in your family is very tall and you'd like your cabinets built higher and deeper than the standard dimensions. That's fine too. And even if you want standard sizes made from a relatively common material, having your cabinets custom-made is still the ideal option. Your architect, kitchen designer, or cabinetmaker can draw up a plan for the cabinets that perfectly matches the style and layout of your kitchen. The one-of-a-kind results will completely satisfy your kitchen dreams and suit your lifestyle, in much the same way that tailor-made garments fit and look so much better than off-the-rack clothing.

Custom cabinets are made using the best construction techniques, and you get a practically unlimited choice of woods, door styles, and moldings as well as paints, glazes, or stains. Going the custom route is pricy, though, and it requires planning ahead since it can take 3 months to 6 months to get your cabinets.

facing page • This kitchen is outfitted with full-overlay doors on frameless cabinetry. The refined style of the cabinet doors and brushed-metal hardware, the wall cabinets with glass doors, and wood molding around the perimeter of the room convey a classic, traditional style.

top and bottom • Appliances get hidden away behind a bifold door. Appliance garages are a great way to keep often-used things at your fingertips without them being scattered across the countertop.

DETAILS THAT WORK

Built-In Door Storage

Who would have thought that a shallow shelving unit could provide privacy, too? Here, a double pocket door installed between the kitchen and the dining room is fitted with shelves for storing culinary goods. This type of clever system requires careful planning during the framing stage so that the appropriate hardware is used to accommodate the depth of the doors.

A Well-Equipped Cook's Kitchen

Having always wanted to live by the ocean, the homeowners couldn't walk away from a seaside cottage that had seen better days. The small house was in disrepair, but it sat on an incredible piece of property. The couple decided to buy the cottage, tear it down, and start from scratch. Although town zoning regulations restricted them to building within the original footprint of the small structure, they were able to add a second story. To meet their needs, they decided to design the house like a boat: incredibly compact.

The owners both love to cook and wanted a well-equipped kitchen with large, high-end appliances. The challenge would be to make this happen in a 12-ft. by 12-ft. space. To maximize storage capacity, the cabinetry was built to reach the 9-ft.-high bead-board ceilings. The open shelves and glass doors on the cabinets add a sense of spaciousness to the room and provide visual texture. Narrow full-height, pull-out storage cabinets were installed on each side of the 48-in. refrigerator. Alongside the sink base, disguised to look like apothecary drawers, are narrow cabinets for grouping trays and other flat items. Pull-out shelves under the sink provide additional storage.

Despite its modest size, the ocean blue center island with a butcher-block top packs in a lot of extra space, too. A rack holds large pots and pans, and built-in wine storage can handle approximately 15 bottles. The owners even managed to squeeze in a flat-screen TV over the top sash of a double-hung window. Not a square inch in this kitchen was overlooked.

left • Narrow pull-out storage units on either side of the refrigerator take advantage of the smallest of spaces. Glass doors on the cabinetry above the refrigerator provide a sense of roominess since the eye is drawn to the back of the cabinet.

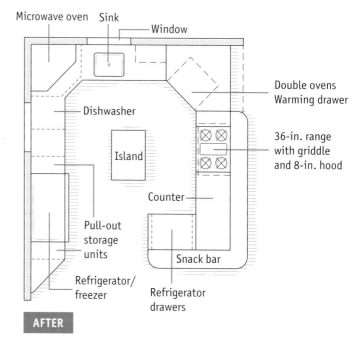

AFTER

Thinking like boat designers, the owners were able to accommodate large professional-style appliances and plenty of handsome storage in a compact space. The center island, though small in size, includes a wine rack and an area for keeping pots and pans at hand.

STOCK

The standardized cabinetry boxes that lumberyards and home centers sell provide relatively quick and inexpensive alternatives to custom-built woodwork. You'll have to make do with modular cabinets in available sizes (they usually come in 3-in. increments), and you'll have limited choices of wood finishes (typically red oak, white birch, and maple) and door styles. Also, many stock cabinets are constructed of low-quality particleboard covered with a vinyl face that's imprinted with a photographic image of wood grain. You'll get better results if you look for premium stock products made of MDF with real wood faces and doors for which optional moldings and pull-out organizers are available.

Working with Windows

Wall-to-wall windows are a beautiful feature in any room. But large expanses of glass limit the amount of wall cabinets that would normally provide storage for glasses and dishes. By installing three shallow shelves across each bank of windows, the owner of this kitchen created additional storage space for her collection of serving items without interfering with the pleasing natural light streaming into the space.

Make sure to buy stock cabinets from a supplier that has the exact products that you're considering out on the display floor, so that you can inspect the model units very carefully. Don't be gentle with the display models. Yank on the doors and drawers—just as your family will when the cabinets are installed in your kitchen. And be aware that, although they're called stock cabinets, these products usually aren't stocked at the retailer but are stored at large regional warehouses; you're likely to wait up to a month for delivery.

One kind of stock cabinets, however, really is stocked at the home center. Called either knock-down or ready-to-assemble cabinets, these come as piles of precut boards with the necessary hardware and instructions for putting them together. That means they fit into relatively small packing boxes, which saves manufacturers money in shipping and makes them the least costly options to buy. They're so compact, in fact, that home centers can stock them on their shelves, and you can take them home with you the same day. Although knock-down cabinets tend to be constructed of lower-quality materials, some of them are quite nice looking, considering their budget-friendly price tags. And spending a weekend or two assembling your own boxes can save you a considerable amount of money.

facing page • Warm cherry and hard maple custom cabinetry harmonize to celebrate the Arts and Crafts style of this kitchen. Using two different wood types in a kitchen design draws attention to the shape and style of the cabinets.

left • Corner cabinets are an efficient way to pack a lot of storage into a small space. A lazy Susan or stacking unit allows you to get into the deepest of corners.

Cabinet Materials

Kitchen cabinetry is a long-term investment. Keep this in mind when choosing a cabinet material for your doors and drawer fronts. The material not only should be durable, offering you years of service, but also should add aesthetic value to your room. Ultimately, which material will work best for you depends on your taste, lifestyle, and, of course, your budget.

MDF
$

- Strong, stable material.
- Takes paint beautifully.
- Unlike wood, can have an unnatural appearance.
- May off-gas urea-formaldehyde, a volatile organic compound (VOC).

LAMINATE
$

- Available in a range of colors, patterns, and textures.
- Easy to clean.
- Fingerprints and smudges show up on surface.
- Difficult to repair chips and scratches.

SOLID WOOD
$$

- Can be stained or have clear finish applied to highlight its warmth and natural beauty.
- Available in a variety of species, including oak, maple, pine, and cherry.
- Natural grain disguises fingerprints and everyday smudges.
- Easy to repair.

LAMINATE

GLASS DOORS
$$–$$$

- Come in a variety of colors and textures.
- Clear glass can give the illusion of spaciousness.
- Interior of cabinet should match exterior finish.
- Glass panels can sometimes rattle within their frames when doors are opened and closed.

STAINLESS STEEL
$$$

- Durable and long lasting.
- Provides a sleek, contemporary look.
- Shows fingerprints and smudges.
- Large expanses in a polished finish can convey a cold, sterile feeling.

STAINLESS STEEL

GLASS DOORS

SOLID WOOD

SEMICUSTOM

As is so often the case, the middle ground is the best option for many people. Like stock products, semicustom cabinets are mass-produced in factories and come in modular sizes. But unlike stock units, you have a whole host of optional upgrades to select from. You can choose boxes made of MDF or plywood, dovetailed drawer joints (which look like interlocking teeth of wood), and real wood doors in a wide range of styles, instead of vinyl-coated look-alikes. And you can choose from a wider range of wood species and a host of optional moldings and convenience accessories. You'll likely wait 6 weeks to 10 weeks for delivery; but, in many cases, the quality far outshines most stock products.

DETAILS THAT WORK

A Custom Cat House

Wanting to take advantage of every square inch of their island and to accommodate every family member, including those covered in fur, the homeowners of this kitchen commissioned a built-in kitty condo, complete with a mullioned window. Pets can sleep undisturbed in a space like this. And the bonus for you? You don't have to look at the pet's bedding. A custom pet house may deter your cat or dog from curling up on your sofa, too.

above · Unique hardware can make many cabinets feel more custom than they really are.

left · Due to its simple styling, traditional frame-and-panel cabinetry can be paired successfully with eclectic components. The hood, round butcher-block storage corner, and exquisite backsplash are the standout features of this kitchen.

facing page · Install storage organizers in unlikely places. What appears as a decorative panel below the pilaster in this custom kitchen is really a handy pull-out drawer for storing spices.

Knobs, Pulls, and Slides

Though cabinet hardware might seem like an afterthought, it can have a big effect on the look and efficiency of your cabinets. Choose 1930s-style crescent-shaped colored glass pulls, for example, and you'll bring a playful retro look to your kitchen, or go with a stainless-steel towel-bar pull and broadcast up-to-the-minute contemporary. And because they are the part of the cabinet that you handle, knobs and pulls should be not only beautiful but comfortable and ergonomic as well. Always test drive hardware in the store to see how it feels.

It is not surprising that heavy, well-designed pieces are likely to feel best in your hand, and it is not surprising that they tend to be the priciest, too. Still, since you probably don't need all that many knobs and pulls for your kitchen, investing in expensive ones can actually be a great way to dress up the kitchen without breaking the bank.

Though they don't share the limelight with knobs and pulls, slides are also important components of the cabinets. Standard slides allow for the drawer to roll only partially out of the base, so ask for full-extension slides, which make it easy to access every inch of the drawer. Another option is bottom-mounted slides, which are hidden from view, allowing the beauty of well-made drawers to be seen and offering a very sophisticated and traditional look. A further upgrade you might want to consider is soft-closing slides, which prevent the drawers from slamming. Not only will they keep things quieter in the kitchen but they will prevent little fingers from accidentally being hurt by a closing drawer. Whatever kind of slides you get, make sure that they're rated for at least 75 lb., meaning they'll hold up to heavy use.

above • Straightforward and simple in design, these pulls and knobs in polished metal complement the traditional style of this serene kitchen in a soft green hue.

left • Square pulls are the right choice for this kitchen with its geometric forms. The pulls in a metal finish echo the boxy shape of the red cabinets while complementing the stainless-steel range and hood.

right • Three different kinds of hardware were used on the cabinetry in this kitchen. The result? The varied styles create an appealing visual mix. The dark finish of each piece of hardware stands out well against the light, naturally finished wood cabinets.

Knobs and Pulls

Despite their basic function and rather diminutive size, knobs and pulls play a relatively large role in the kitchen. Visible to the eye, they add character to cabinetry and help define the style of your room. Contemporary hardware is available in an assortment of materials, finishes, and shapes. You can find everything from colored glass and ceramics to hand-crafted metal fashioned in the shape of utensils, twigs, and even starfish.

1. To underscore the country style theme of the kitchen, the homeowner chose simple porcelain knobs to adorn the pine cabinetry. The hardware ties in with the all-white countertop and stove. 2. This traditional white cabinetry gets a visual boost from textural knobs in a rust finish. The hardware sets off the granite countertops and backsplash as well as the cabinet's decorative trim. 3. Pulls in brushed nickel stand out beautifully against the stained cherry cabinets in this rich, warm kitchen. The high-gloss finish of the pulls harmonizes with the gleaming cooktop and hood.

4. The hardware on this contemporary-style cabinetry adds an informal, roughhewn element to the kitchen. Had the hardware been more refined in its design, the space would have gained a sleeker and more sophisticated feel. **5.** Sculptural pulls add an artistic element to this cabinet. Their bronze metal finish complements the warm wood beautifully, and their size is the perfect scale for the long, narrow surface. **6.** No detail was left behind in this room. Pulls and knobs—even those behind cabinet doors—match to create a unified feeling throughout the whole kitchen.

Maximize Storage

Nothing is more frustrating to a cook than having to search out a missing ingredient hiding in the back of a shelf or to unload stacks of mixing bowls to reach the electric mixer stowed in a corner cabinet. But if you plan your cabinets right, you'll never have those struggles again. There are two keys to organized kitchen storage: having plenty of cabinets and outfitting them with accessories that make it easy to access their depths.

To maximize the cabinet space in your kitchen plan, consider going beyond a row of base and wall cabinets along two or three walls. An island or peninsula can add large storage compartments to the center of the kitchen—where drawers, doors, and cubbies can provide convenient access to items such as cutting boards and trash cans. A deep floor-to-ceiling pantry cabinet is ideal for storing food supplies. Or you can create a built-in hutch for your tableware using base cabinets and extra-tall wall cabinets with glass doors.

above • To maximize storage, cabinets were built to the 10-ft. ceiling. Only 8 in. of wall space remained after fitting the refrigerator and microwave oven, so a shallow but very useful tall pantry was designed to hold an amazing amount of kitchen provisions.

below • Pull-out shelving is a wonderful accessory for narrow base cabinets. Short side walls on each of the four shelves hold canned goods and small items in place and do not interfere with your view of the labels.

above • Space above the refrigerator has traditionally been underused. This pop up storage cabinet has no center stile, so large serving platters are easily stored and pulled down for use.

A former doorway in this vintage-style kitchen serves a new function with the addition of wallboard and a few sturdy shelves. The built-in feature adds charm to the room and creates additional space for displaying wares.

Plentiful Storage in a Small Space

A 230-year-old Massachusetts house lured a culinary publicist and literary agent to begin extensive renovations to suit her professional needs. Because her work often involved bringing several professional chefs together for training, she knew she needed a kitchen that would perform well. Her goal was to outfit the space with enough equipment and storage to accommodate up to 12 people cooking all at once.

To handle cooking and prep work, a six-burner range and two separate sink areas, each capable of cleanup duty, were installed. Finding extra counter space was a challenge, though. To almost double the amount of work surfaces in the kitchen, pull-out wood chopping boards that lock into place were installed in the top rail of almost every base cabinet. When not in use, they neatly tuck away out of sight. Cherry cabinets designed with hinged spice racks that open separately from the door provide adequate room for storing numerous jars of spices. The hinged rack holds small jars on both sides and, when opened, reveals an additional row of shelves behind it. An abundance of vertical tray and platter storage dividers in the kitchen are used for storing anything flat and large. The result is a space that provides room for up to a dozen hardworking cooks.

above • When opened, a bookcase used for keeping the owner's collection of cookbooks in order reveals hidden storage for baking equipment in an extra-deep cabinet.

left • The prep sink area, topped with a granite counter and including a dishwasher, is a reproduction of an old apothecary cabinet. Reaching from floor to ceiling, it's used to store the homeowner's everyday dishes, flatware, and other cooking utensils.

facing page • To get the most out of the kitchen, the homeowner used every inch of cabinet space. Three ample compartments for storing spices are created by the use of a double-sided swinging spice rack with additional storage behind it in a standard-depth wall cabinet.

To make the most of your cabinets, look for products such as roll-out trays, which are shallow drawers that hide behind cabinet doors and make small items like pastas and canned goods accessible, even when they're stashed deep in the cabinet. Drawer baskets offer open-air storage that prolongs the shelf life of foodstuffs like potatoes and onions. And there are recycling bins; spice racks; pop-up mixing stands; and a host of other racks, dividers, and shelves that will keep your cooking supplies right at your fingertips whenever you need them.

top • In a place where a countertop would occasionally come in handy, a pull-out between the upper and the lower cabinets provides a temporary resting place for dishes and boosts the efficiency level of the kitchen.

above • This magnetized knife holder has a mesh metal face to protect knife blades and fingers. If you have small children in the house, be mindful of the location of storage for cutlery and fragile items.

left • If you don't have space for a walk-in pantry, reconfigure a built-in cabinet to take its place. Combine standard shelves with shallower ones attached to the back of the cabinet doors and add deep bulk-storage drawers or pull-out shelves to hold foodstuffs of all sizes.

Hiding Command Central

When a busy northern New Jersey family decided it was time for a kitchen renovation, their goals were simple. Of course, they wanted state-of-the-art appliances and beautiful cabinetry, but they also needed space for handling the calendars, Little League schedules, car pool schedules, dentist appointments, bills, and other stuff that comes in the mail and out of backpacks and briefcases. They needed a "command central" for their home, and the kitchen was the logical place for it.

Cleverly hidden behind doors in an extra-deep wall cabinet is a system of drawers and dividers that helps keep the family organized. Three small apothecary drawers hold postage stamps, rubber bands, paper clips, school lunch money, and the like. Cell phone and camera chargers are on a shelf with an electrical outlet. Incoming and outgoing mail sit in individual cubbies, and important books have a place to stand up. Corkboard was fastened to the back of the doors to hold schedules, appointment cards, and favorite photos. Under the cabinetry is a four-in-one electronic device: It's a DVD player, radio, and TV that offers Internet access. The screen flips up when not it use and the keyboard fits nicely into a base drawer. When the doors of this command hub are closed, no one would ever suspect the workhorse that exists behind them.

top • When the cabinet doors are closed, no one would suspect that there was a home office in this formal kitchen. This is a great way to incorporate a desk without the look of a work area, even in a limited space.

bottom • Cabinet dividers, apothecary drawers, and careful planning help the homeowners organize the inevitable paper clutter. Corkboard fastened to the doors holds family schedules, phone numbers, and favorite photos.

Storage

Gone are the days when kitchen storage amounted to nothing more than a short row of cabinets, a few narrow drawers, and— if you were lucky—a lazy Susan. Now there are pull-out shelves for canned goods, handy organizers for trash and recycling receptacles, and drawer inserts for spices and flatware. Today's storage options do their part in keeping the kitchen tidy and running smoothly.

1. These small built-in square shelves do more than provide handy storage for bottles of wine: Their uniform design also adds interest and pattern to the room. 2. Many types of pull-out bins and shelves are available through home centers and home stores and can be retrofitted to existing cabinetry. 3. Don't overlook the backsplash behind the stove or cooktop as a place for storing utensils and kitchen gadgets. Here, a thin stainless-steel rod creates additional space for hanging a colander and bottle opener and for keeping cooking wine close at hand. 4. Available in stainless steel or plastic, a tilt-out tray installed in front of a kitchen sink provides adequate storage space for cleaning scrubbers and sponges.

5. Each baking piece has its place in this deep base cabinet. Two shelves hold small to medium baking gear. Larger cookie sheets are in their own cabinet. **6.** Get the most storage space out of a cabinet by installing a vertical divider to keep narrow items orderly. Lazy Susans are another good alternative; their rotating discs eliminate the need to reach into the depths of the cabinets. **7.** Keep kitchen linens handy with a pull-out towel bar. Install this type of feature under the sink or in a small base cabinet near your primary cleanup area.

COUNTERTOPS

Countertops—along with their vertical neighbors, backsplashes—

are the frosting on the cake, bringing swaths of color and texture to kitchens.

From a cooking point of view, though, they're utilitarian work surfaces.

AND

So in addition to choosing the look you want,

you need to consider the way you'll use your kitchen and how much

abuse your countertops are likely to face.

BACKSPLASHES

Materials

Before we get to all of the countertop and backsplash materials that are available these days, think about this: You don't have to choose only one. Backsplashes and countertops need not be made from the same materials. And it's even possible to put different countertop surfaces in different work zones—such as something very durable in a spot designed for food prep and something more fragile and decorative in an area used primarily for storage. Or you might use a costly countertop in a highly visible area, such as a breakfast bar island, and something more moderately priced for your other counters.

above · A strip of mosaic tiles add sizzle to a simple 4 in. by 4 in. tile backsplash. The Art Deco theme is repeated on the countertop by pairing a light surface material with a contrasting black edge.

top facing page · The vintage style of this kitchen is underscored by the richly colored wood countertop and the farmhouse-style sink. To protect the wood from damaging spills and splashes, the material must be sealed periodically.

bottom facing page · A field of earthy clay tiles placed on a diagonal, frame an arrangement of 4 hand painted porcelain tiles. An ogee shaped stone frame around the tiles allow for the transition from $^3/_8$ in. to $^5/_8$ in. tile.

Countertop, backsplash, and floor share the same color family, making the cabinets the focal point of this kitchen.

top · The rich colors of glazed field tiles and matching band of accent tiles nicely tie together the tones of the countertop, wood cabinets, and stainless appliances.

bottom · Countertops with a decorative deep ogee edge treatment add unique character. Here the widely cut edge works well on the beautiful stone and complements the traditional styling of the cabinets.

right · A combination of concrete and stainless-steel give the countertops in this kitchen a similar feel of color. Together they add quiet areas to complement the highly patterned backsplash.

far right facing page · White subway tiles paired with the wood countertop create a clean, vintage look in this kitchen.

For that matter, countertops and backsplashes are fairly easy to swap out later—an upscale countertop can cost more than $5,000 for a standard-size kitchen (say, a 10-ft. by 11-ft. L-shaped kitchen with 3-ft. by 6-ft. island). So if your renovation budget is tight, you might consider holding off on the countertop of your dreams. If you can muster the patience, you might install a simple, economical countertop now. Then, someday when your finances allow, you can replace it with a more up-to-date material, with very little mess or hassle.

Because backsplashes aren't work surfaces, however, you actually have many additional choices for them, from old-fashioned "tin" ceiling tiles to translucent glass mosaics to beaded-board wainscot. Just be sure the part of the backsplash that sits directly on your countertop is durable and moisture resistant. Less-durable material, like wainscot, should sit atop a 2-in.- to 4-in.-high stone splash or other durable surface so that it can't wick up any countertop spills.

Countertops

The most important factor in choosing a countertop surface is durability. Materials need to hold up against heat, moisture, and food—especially acidic kinds. Special care must be given to any surface installed around a sink, too. In addition to being hard wearing, a countertop also should add aesthetic value to your kitchen.

CONCRETE

LAMINATE

LAMINATE

$

- Available in a range of colors and patterns that mimic the look of stone and wood.
- Fast and easy installation.
- Nonresistant to scratches and heat.
- Excessive moisture in seams can degrade the substrate.
- Has a relatively short lifespan.

STONE

$$$

- Beautiful selection of natural colors and textures.
- Hard and durable; resists scratches, chips, and heat.
- Available in a polished or honed (matte) finish.
- Fits well in both traditional and contemporary settings.
- Must be sealed regularly against staining.

TILE

$$

- Vast assortment of colors, surface textures, and sizes allow for unmatched design flexibility.
- Resistant to heat.
- Glazed tile is not affected by water; unglazed tile must be sealed, as do grout lines.
- Complex installation process.
- Grouted joints can crack, stain, and create uneven surfaces.

SOLID SURFACE

$$$

- Wide array of color and pattern options.
- Features seamless edge details and integrated sinks.
- Resistant to stains and moisture.
- Surface can be renewed with sanding or scouring.
- Can crack or burn if exposed to high heat.

WOOD

STAINLESS STEEL

$$–$$$

- Durable, hygienic, and long-lasting.
- Heat, water, and stain resistant.
- Easy to clean.
- Shows fingerprints and scratches; dulls knives.
- Capable of denting.

WOOD

$$–$$$

- Adds warmth and natural beauty to kitchens.
- Can be stained or left natural.

- Scratches, scorches, and stains can be sanded away or left for character.
- Won't dull knives.
- Requires sealing against moisture.

CONCRETE

$$$

- Broad variety of colors and finishes.
- Pliability allows for an assortment of shapes and decorative applications.
- Adds a one-of-kind look to kitchens.
- Can scratch and crack.
- Must be sealed to avoid stains.

TILE

SOLID SURFACE

STAINLESS STEEL

STONE

STONE

No two stone countertops look exactly alike because no two stones are identical. The veins, speckles, and mineral deposits on the surface of granite, limestone, and marble are as varied and eye catching as nature itself. Stone is one of the toughest countertop materials, but it needs to be immune to standing water, hot pans, and knife blades. One more caveat: The acids in everyday liquids such as coffee, vinegar, fruit juice, wine, and even ketchup are harmful to all stones, some more than others. A limestone, marble, or soapstone counter will literally dissolve a little bit wherever it comes in contact with one of these acids—and it'll happen faster than you can wipe up the puddle. So if you choose stone, regular sealing is essential (though minor acid damage won't be too noticeable and conspicuous problems can often be repaired by a professional). Or you can use granite, the gold standard for countertops, which is affected far less by food acids. In any case, you'll need to ask your stone seller for a piece that's suitable for kitchen countertop use; he or she can also tell you how often you'll need to seal the counters to keep them protected.

A custom-cut slab of stone is one of the priciest countertop options, but stone tiles offer a similar look for about half of the cost of a one-piece counter in the same type of stone. Just pick tiles without much "activity"—the term for veins and flecks that appear on the surface—so they'll match up nicely, and use a color-matched grout, and you'll get the beauty and durability of stone for a bargain price.

top right • It's best to have at least 18 in. of countertop on one side of a cooktop and at least 36 in. on the other to allow adequate space for meal preparation.

right • Handmade tiles add subtle color to the stone sink and countertop in this kitchen.

facing page • Dropping the height by as little as 1½ in. between two or more countertops is a great way to avoid a seam in a stone counter. This split-level granite counter also boasts an overhang, allowing for a stool to be pulled up to the work surface.

A Swirling Stone Pattern Captures the Eye

The new owners of this contemporary-style home were immediately drawn to the high ceilings in this kitchen. The original design of the room, however, didn't work. The sink was positioned in front of the window alongside a dishwasher. And the island, outfitted with an oversize cooktop, lacked an overhang, preventing guests from cozying up to the area for meals and conversation. Because the kitchen opened up to a formal living room, its new design had to complement the adjoining space as well as harmonize with the owners' refined taste in furnishings.

So that the cavernous ceiling in the kitchen would serve as an architectural focal point, but not draw attention away from the lower portion of the room, the owners chose granite slabs with a stunning vein of color for the countertops and the backsplash. Paired with cabinetry in a subtle, sophisticated gray, the watercolor-like pattern of the stone holds its own, providing a striking visual counterbalance to the soaring ceiling. Hardware in a brushed metal finish ties in with the stainless-steel range, hood, and sink, which was moved to the island to allow the cook to interact with guests in the adjacent living area.

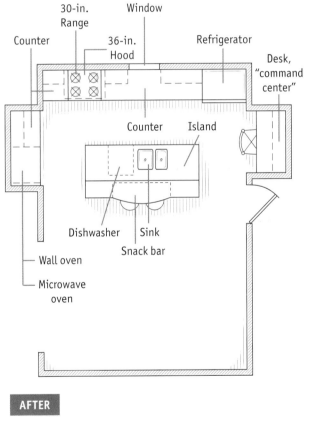

far left facing page · To strike a visual balance between the upper and the lower portions of this contemporary space, the homeowners paired cabinetry in a subtle shade with highly patterned granite. The result? The eye is arrested by the stone but also captivated by the room's soaring ceiling, which serves as an architectural focal point.

left · Polished granite becomes a stunning centerpiece as a full-height backsplash. This slab of stone was chosen specifically for this area. The cabinets on either side of the backsplash plus the hood above frame the swirling pattern beautifully.

30-in. Range

Window

Counter

36-in. Hood

Refrigerator

Desk, "command center"

Counter

Island

Dishwasher

Sink

Snack bar

Wall oven

Microwave oven

AFTER

WOOD

Wood was the original countertop material, and it has become popular once again because of its natural beauty and today's extremely durable clear finishes. Also, wood is gentle on breakables and won't dull your knives. It will need regular oiling, however, to keep it from drying out. And it's at risk of injury from knives, hot pans, and standing water, although damage often can be sanded out. Most wood countertops are made from maple, often in a butcher block format, which consists of narrow strips of wood that are glued together to form a very strong and durable surface. Teak, mahogany, cherry, alder, and walnut are also available, however, and offer deeper tones and richer grain patterns.

top right • The standard thickness of butcher block is 1½ in., although thicker tops are available such as this 4-in.-thick counter. The benefits of butcher block are many: It's easy to install, it's resilient, and it can be used as a cutting board.

bottom right • The drop-in ceramic sink, pillowed subway tiles, and wide trim on the window contribute to the vintage feel of this cottage kitchen.

facing page • Mahogany countertops and shelving provide a warm contrast to the all-white cabinets in this butler's pantry. Since heat and moisture from appliances and sinks may potentially harm the stability of wood, this application is ideal.

DETAILS THAT WORK

A Built-In Drain Board

The owners of this kitchen didn't want an unsightly plastic drain mat obscuring this rich teak countertop, so they commissioned a drain board, a sculpted area of grooves that drains water into a sink. The functional design celebrates the beauty and practicality of this hardwood, which has natural water-shedding resins. Although some hardwoods are well suited for drain boards, concrete and stone are other possible options. Any material but solid-surface acrylics, however, will require periodic sealing against long-term exposure to water.

CONCRETE

A concrete countertop is nothing like a sidewalk. For one thing, the special blend of concrete that's used is very fine and pure, resulting in an ultra-smooth, stone-like finish. For another, you can have pigments added to the wet mix (or have it stained after it has cured) to create a countertop in any color you like. And you can have objects such as shells, stones, or colored glass added to the wet surface, which later gets polished as smooth as terrazzo. Plus, concrete can be poured into virtually any custom shape that you want. The resulting surfaces are as strong as stone; however, they are extremely porous, so frequent sealing is required to prevent the surface from darkening and staining. You also need to be prepared to see hairline cracks, which are harmless but can look like flaws to the uninitiated.

above • A cast concrete island tinted with a brilliant sky blue pigment resembles actual blue stone. The color of the counter fits well in this kitchen, reinforcing the room's cool feel.

right • This solid block of concrete provides strong structural support for the concrete counter in a polished finish. The exposed vertical surface of the island base also adds texture to the space.

far right facing page • Concrete can be left its natural gray hue or dyed to almost any color, such as red or green.

Customized Concrete Countertop

Concrete in and of itself is a unique choice for a kitchen countertop, but it can also be tinted to almost any color or stained, stamped, stenciled, or polished. The material is incredibly malleable, too. You can shape it into sharp angles or smooth curves and imbed it with objects such as river stones, seashells, or—as shown here—fossils. The result is a personalized, one-of-a-kind look. Almost any durable item can be imbedded into a concrete countertop before it cures.

STAINLESS STEEL

There are good reasons why so many restaurants use stainless steel for their kitchen countertops: It's tough, easy to clean, and won't be harmed by spills or hot pans. It will, however, change over time. Dents and dings will appear and so will water spots, stains, and fingerprints. If you can view those changes as enhancements to the countertop's beauty, then stainless is an excellent option. But if every mark will cause you anguish, this is not the countertop for you. Also, if you're planning to install stainless-steel appliances, using the same material on the countertops might simply be too much of a good thing.

SOLID SURFACE

Solid surface countertops are most often referred to as Corian®, though that's just one of the brands of solid surfacing that you can get. Solid-surface countertops are made from acrylic polymers (which are basically just high-grade plastics) often mixed with particles of natural stone before being custom molded for your job. The result is a one-piece countertop, often without any visible seams, that can even have an integral sink made from the same material. Solid surfacing is available in hundreds of colors, including speckled faux stone looks. The work surface won't be harmed by spills—neither the acidic sort nor the potentially staining sort. And while it can get scratched by knives or scorched by hot pans, the damage often can be sanded out.

top • A butler's pantry deserves the same style that's applied to the kitchen. The combination of painted cabinets, sink with large apron, stone countertop, and traditional-style backsplash tiles makes this space feel larger than it is, thanks to the cohesiveness of the styling.

above • Stainless steel is a durable, low-maintenance material for countertops. When paired with the right cabinets and accessories it doesn't feel out of place.

left • Highly polished countertops reflect a lot of light. Here they complement the unique copper backsplash, mirroring that material's sheen without taking away any of its punch.

facing page • This strategically placed window of glass block extends the short limestone backsplash. The window, impervious to splashes, also provides a shallow ledge and allows sunlight to fill the space.

A Remodeled Kitchen Serves Up Extra Space

A poorly designed kitchen that didn't appeal to the new owners of this 1958 center-hall colonial fueled a complete renovation. The original kitchen felt cramped thanks to a large column in the middle of the room and an ill-placed double oven that blocked the view to the outside. In addition, the oven was the first thing guests saw when they walked into the front door of the house. The aim of the overhaul was to open up the space and make room for multiple cooks to work as well for family and friends to gather.

The column was removed, and a wall cabinet with glass doors took the place of the double oven, which was moved to the other side of the room; a warming drawer, storage, and a hidden microwave also were added. Since the space required multiple counters to accommodate more than one cook, a mix of countertop surfaces was used. The maple island adds warmth to the room while the curved butternut top on the island bar invites guests to collect and socialize.

above • A curved top was added to the center island to encourage family and friends to sit and stay a while. The rounded shape adds visual appeal to the room as does its warm butternut surface and front, which play off of the maple-topped island and nearby countertops.

facing page • To draw attention to the butcher block countertop and the island base, the designer of this space used two contrasting wood types: light maple and dark butternut. The combination attracts the eye both to the top and the bottom portions of this handsome, hardworking piece.

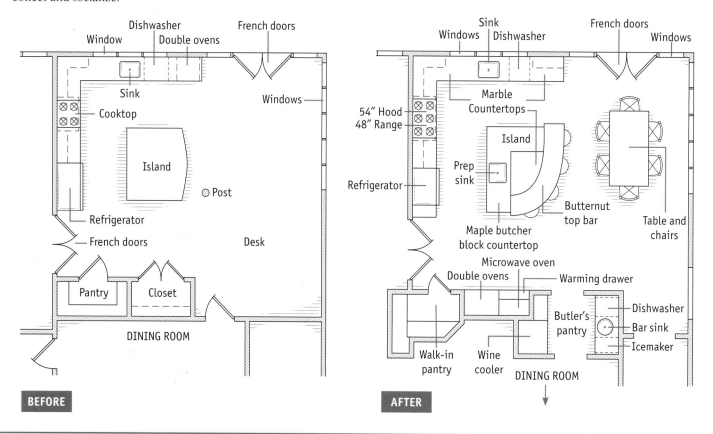

CERAMIC TILE

Tile offers perhaps the greatest potential for creating something truly one of a kind—there is a great variety of ceramic tile, the tiles can be mixed and matched, and they can be laid in a nearly infinite number of different patterns. What's more, quality countertop tile is immune to damage from knives, spills, and bubbling hot casseroles set down without trivets. Just make sure to ask your supplier for tile that's tough enough for countertop duty. Hard-glazed tiles make for easier-to-clean counters than unglazed tiles do; but with routine sealing, even unglazed ceramic is a durable option.

above • Stamped metal tiles set in a field of larger stone tiles create a simple, yet appealing backsplash design. In addition, the warm color of the accent tile complements the wood cabinetry.

left • Tile comes in a broad range of materials, including metal, concrete, stone, and glass. Creating a custom pattern like this one is a labor-intensive process. It requires the installer to cut the field tiles so that the accent tiles fit neatly in place.

right • There's nothing overdone about this brick tile backsplash. The tiles were laid in straight rows with alternating joints.

Another possibility is porcelain tile, which can be as tough as granite and comes in a wide array of faux looks, from stone to glazed ceramic tile. You can mix in some accent tiles—perhaps handmade Arts and Crafts tiles or embossed stainless-steel ones—to dress up a field of plainer tiles. And you can treat the edges with special rounded or ogee-shaped trim tiles or with wood or metal edging sold for that purpose.

The big maintenance issue with tile countertops is the grout, which can be difficult to clean. You can minimize this problem by using large tiles to reduce the number of grout lines that you have; asking the installer to lay the tiles as close together as possible to keep the grout lines thin; and selecting an epoxy grout, which is much stronger than standard grout, needs far less sealing, and resists staining. (Note, however, that all grout and many tiles should be sealed.)

above • Soft, subtle colors work well in this Craftsman-style kitchen. The handmade wheat-motif tiles in the backsplash are framed with matching bullnose tile, giving the backsplash more of a centerpiece feeling.

Backsplashes

Kitchen backsplashes serve a dual purpose: They protect your walls from spills and splatters, and they add a surprising amount of visual interest to a relatively small area. Typically, they fill up 16 in. to 18 in. of space behind your sink and prep areas and up to 36 in. behind the range, which allows an additional opportunity for a design statement by way of a mural or contrasting tile pattern. Thoughtfully designed, a backsplash can be a dramatic focal point for your kitchen.

1. In areas where heat and moisture are an issue, choose taller backsplashes to protect plaster or drywall from damage. Here, earthy colored slate tiles turned on point harmonize with the red birch cabinetry and black granite countertop.
2. Tile is an ideal choice for a backsplash since it's heat resistant and can be sealed against moisture. It's also a stylish option, adding a layer of color and pattern to any kitchen design. **3.** The colors and textures of your backsplash should blend or contrast with your cabinetry and your countertops. Paired with crisp white cabinetry, this soapstone backsplash makes a strong statement.
4. The arched tile design above the cooktop serves as a functional focal point: Its niche draws the eye, and the shallow ledge affords handy storage for seasonings and cooking oils. A band of accent tile running along the outside edge ties the tall, well-used space to the backsplash beneath the wall cabinets.

4

LAMINATE

Though it won't make as much of a design statement as any of the other countertop choices, laminate is practical, watertight, and affordable. Plus, these days you can get laminates that don't look like laminates—they look like stone thanks to photographic images of the real thing just under the clear surface of the material. You can also get laminates (at a higher cost) that are colored all the way through the sheet, which means that there are no dark lines where the edges are exposed and scratches are not readily apparent. And laminates are still the least expensive option, sometimes coming in at about one-tenth the cost of stone or solid surface. Still, these products can get scorched and scratched, and their edges are prone to breakage. Choosing a laminate countertop limits you to a drop-in sink.

far left facing page • A concrete backsplash and countertop tie the work area together. Concrete must be sealed periodically to protect it from stains, particularly when it will be exposed to grease and food from cooking.

left • This bungalow-style kitchen is perfectly accented. Because the walls and countertops have similar colors, the cabinets, light fixtures, and appliances can take center stage

right • Perhaps the greatest allure of tile is its versatility. This backsplash of handcrafted tiles in subtle blue and caramel adds warmth and texture that attracts the eye as well as the hand.

below • Laminate surfaces come in a broad range of colors and patterns, all of which can be fitted with a decorative countertop edge, in wood or stainless steel, for example. Here, a maple edge that matches the kitchen cabinetry complements this countertop in a neutral hue. The result is a thoughtfully designed and attractive work surface.

SINKS

You will use your new sink and faucet for almost every task

you do in the kitchen, from making coffee to scrubbing vegetables

and cleaning up from meals.

AND

So, it's essential that you make sink and faucet choices

that suit your kitchen design, are easy to operate, and will look good

and work well after years of heavy use.

FAUCETS

Sinks

There are two ways to think about sinks—as utilitarian workhorses that leave the decorative punch to the other features of the kitchen or as utilitarian workhorses that bring a visual pizzazz of their own. In other words, whether you go stylized or simple, above all, your sink should be a well-designed kitchen tool. That generally means a broad bowl, sturdy construction, and an easy-to-clean finish. Even the sink's placement will have a major effect on the rest of the kitchen, dictating which cabinets you'll use for your dishes and glasses, where your dishwasher will be installed, and the locations of a host of other kitchen components.

below • Durable and relatively inexpensive, stainless steel is the most popular material for sinks. Choose true stainless steel as opposed to an alloy, and opt for a sink that's at least 18 gauge—it will be quieter and more dent resistant than lower-gauge steel.

above • This custom soapstone sink has two very large bowls with two different depths. With such a large sink, careful consideration must be given to the size and style of the faucet you choose. A wall-mount faucet would have worked well here also.

facing page • Ceramic sinks have made their way from being exclusively bathroom fixtures to gracing kitchens. They can be hand painted to match colors in backsplashes, decorative hardware, and other kitchen details. Drawback: They are at some risk for scratching and chipping.

LOCATION, LOCATION, LOCATION

Your old sink is anchored to its spot by numerous plumbing connections. So when you're planning your remodel, you'll need either to put the new sink in the same location or to be prepared to pay a plumber a sizable fee to move the hot and cold water supplies, drain line, and vent pipe inside your walls. What's more, your sink is probably located in front of a window. You can certainly put the new sink somewhere else and, for example, create a food prep counter in front of the view instead—but wherever you place the sink, you'll need to design some headroom above it; it can't go under a standard bank of wall cabinets.

Even if you stick with the existing sink location, though, you can add another sink somewhere else. In addition to the main full-size cleanup sink, you might consider a smaller food-prep sink, with a disposal, located on an island or in another convenient spot where you'll be doing your chopping and dicing. Or you might include a sink in a bar area near the dining room for serving purposes. Also, keep in mind that any full-size sink should have about 2 ft. of countertop on each side, so you can stack dirty dishes and set a drain board nearby. A prep sink should have a minimum of 3 in. on one side and 18 in. on the other so you can do your chopping within easy reach of the sink, disposal, and faucet.

top • A handy drawer was designed into the apron front of this high-end stainless-steel sink for storing dish sponges and scrubbers. The accompanying gooseneck faucet makes rinsing or filling large pots and pans an easy task.

above • A stainless-steel triple bowl undermount sink requires an extra-large cabinet, 42 in. wide or more. Here, a chrome faucet with a pull-out spray hose, soap dispenser, and hot water dispenser are all at hand. The stone backsplash features a long, wall-mounted organizer.

left • Because of their relatively small size, wet bar sinks can be made with more expensive materials such as brass, copper, or titanium. These metals require extra maintenance, however. Here, a titanium sink with a gooseneck faucet is the perfect fit for this modest wet bar.

facing page • You won't find one of these vintage porcelain enameled sinks at your local home store, but you may happen upon one at an antiques shop, flea market, or renovator's supply store. Have it professionally refinished and add a new wall-mount-style faucet, like the one shown here.

Sink Types

Sinks are made to be mounted by different methods; the most common are undermount, drop in, and integral. Undermount sinks, for which the counter extends over the edge of the sink, are designed for use with solid countertops, such as stone, solid surface, concrete, and stainless steel. Integrated sinks, in which the sink is made of the same material as the counter-tops, offer a sleek look. Drop-in sinks are commonly used with laminate and wood countertops, because the edges of these materials should not be overexposed to moisture.

UNDERMOUNT

$$–$$$

- Neat and tidy appearance.
- Cleanup is easy because you can sweep crumbs and puddled water into the sink without interruption.
- Can be used with solid surface, stone, stainless steel, concrete, and teak countertops.

DROP-IN

$–$$$

- Ideal for moisture-sensitive laminate and wood countertops.
- Need to clean periodically where rim meets countertop.
- Can be used with laminate, solid surface, tile, stone, stainless steel, concrete, and wood countertops.

INTEGRAL

$$–$$$

- Ideal mate to solid-surface countertops.
- Blends seamlessly with countertops.
- Can be used with solid-surface or stainless steel countertops.

INTEGRAL

UNDERMOUNT

UNDERMOUNT

DROP-IN

MOUNTING STYLE

The way your sink gets mounted, which is dictated primarily by the unit you choose, will have major consequences for both appearance and convenience. There are essentially three options, and not all of the sink types will work with all types of countertops. It's a good idea to consider the style of sink you want while you're selecting your countertop.

- *Drop-in sinks* get installed from above the counter-top and have a rim that hangs over it. They've been the standard sink type for a long time, but they have the drawback of creating a hard-to-clean groove around the perimeter of the sink, where food and moisture can collect.

- *Undermount sinks* have no such rim. They sit completely under the countertop, so that there's no seam or ridge in the work surface that borders the sink. The countertop simply continues over the edge of the sink; this means you can sweep crumbs and debris into the sink without encountering any obstacles.

- *Integral sinks* take things a step farther: They're fabricated as one piece with the countertop, so there are no visible seams or joints of any kind, anywhere.

Place a second sink away from the main cleanup and cooking areas to allow two cooks to work independently without crowding. This circular prep sink, which features an instant hot water dispenser, complements the nearby round stool and the lighting fixture above.

above • Locating a sink in a corner can be a very effective use of space, especially in smaller kitchens. On either side of this apron-front sink is a span of uninterrupted counter space for preparing meals and tending to other kitchen-related tasks. A deep, corner shelf installed behind the sink provides extra room.

left • This stainless-steel undermount sink set into a moss green concrete countertop features a built-in drain board. The mix of materials and textures turns the cleanup area into a fetching, eye-catching design element.

A Creative Approach to Sink Placement

In the original kitchen in this post and beam house, the sink was positioned in the traditional location under the window. Because of the narrowness of the U-shaped countertop, the dishwasher had to be placed away from the sink under one of the adjacent counters. The kitchen was divided into two separate areas, and the refrigerator was separated from the sink and cooking appliances. In short, the kitchen was cramped and the layout was awkward and inefficient.

A major change to the floor plan repositioned the sink. Rather than the obligatory under-the-window location, the designer elected to install the sink in one of the countertop's corners. This small move had a big effect. Now, not only do the homeowners still have a view out of the original window but they also have a view out a pair of French doors in the nearby living room. Moving the sink allowed the professional-style cooktop to hug the inside corner, which, in turn, made room for a refrigerator within a desirable smaller work triangle. And now the dishwasher is located just to the right of the sink; the homeowners enjoy using the counter under the window for meal prep.

above • Soft yellow cabinetry, a stainless double oven, and light amber stone counters installed opposite the kitchen window reflect light back into the room. The pale, reflective colors and surfaces are a welcome contrast to the dark post-and-beam ceiling.

left • The expanse of countertop below the window is ideal for prepping meals or stacking dirty dishes. Had the sink been placed in this area, space for the professional-style cooktop would have been compromised.

facing page • Installing the sink kitty-corner allows the homeowner to have a view out of the original window but also enjoy the view out of a pair of French doors in the adjacent living room.

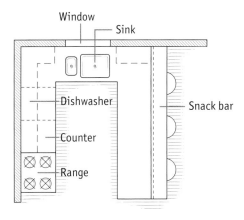

Window
Sink
Dishwasher
Snack bar
Counter
Range

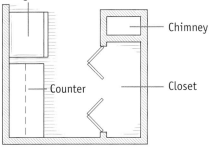

Refrigerator
Chimney
Counter
Closet

BEFORE

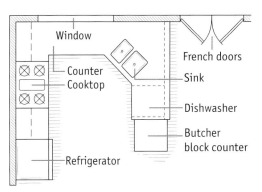

Window
French doors
Counter
Cooktop
Sink
Dishwasher
Butcher block counter
Refrigerator

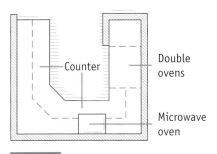

Counter
Double ovens
Microwave oven

AFTER

HOW MANY BOWLS?

A basic kitchen sink is nothing more than a square or rectangular bowl with a drain at the bottom. But there are other configurations that you can consider, including stylized bowl shapes and two- and three-bowl sinks. The idea behind multiple bowls is that they allow you to multitask—using one side for soapy water and the other for rinsing the dishes, for example, or filling a pot with water in one while you're peeling vegetables for your soup in the other.

If that kind of versatility appeals to you, you may want a multi-bowl sink. But consider this: To effectively wash large pots and serving dishes, you'll need a bowl that's at least 20 in. by 17 in. (and 7 in. deep, though you can make up for a shallower bowl with a high gooseneck faucet). To meet that size requirement with a multibowl sink generally means choosing a unit that has one large bowl and one small one, rather than two of equal size. (Three-bowl sinks almost never include any bowl that's large enough for pot-washing.) And any two-bowl sink is going to require a wide sink base (the cabinet that holds it), which means less room for other things in your kitchen.

Built-In Conveniences

When choosing your sink, also consider selecting a dispenser for hot water or liquid dishwashing soap. Hot water dispensers can save you time preparing hot beverages and soups or thawing frozen foods. Soap dispensers streamline the efficiency of your sink area, reducing clutter.

Typically you'll purchase dispensers along with your faucet, so you're sure the style and finish of each fixture match. Holes for dispensers are fabricated in your countertop at the time your faucet is installed or, in the case of stone or stainless countertops, during fabrication. A hot water dispenser plugs into an electrical outlet installed under the sink, because it requires water connections a plumber should install it. A dispenser for soap, however, can be put in by anyone, once the countertop fabricator has drilled the hole.

top • A single-hole brushed nickel gooseneck faucet is located on the divider of this stone sink, ensuring that the faucet will swing into both bowls. Separate lotion and soap dispensers are neat and tidy, keeping large bottles of washing liquid off the sleek counter.

above • Dispensers for hot water and liquid soap can add convenience to the kitchen. Holes for each of these fixtures were cut into the granite countertop during the fabrication process.

facing page • Small island prep sinks are a great way to reduce congestion at the main work areas of the kitchen.

MATERIALS

And then, of course, comes the big question: What sink material do you want? The choices abound, from the mirror-like polish of stainless steel to the rich earthen textures of natural stone.

STAINLESS STEEL

By far the most popular choice is stainless steel, because it's durable, hides scratches and dents, and is relatively inexpensive. Look for true stainless steel instead of a lower-cost alloy and for a sink that's at least 18 gauge—a measure of its thickness, for which the number gets *lower* as the thickness *increases*—because it will be quieter and more dent resistant than lower-quality products. (Commercial-grade or professional-style sinks, which are also available for home use, are typically 16 gauge.) Matte finishes are better at hiding scratches than high-shine ones, and you can get a sink with a plastic coating on the underside to dampen the sounds of the water as it bounces off the bottom.

Garbage Disposals

Garbage disposals can be a handy and mess-free way to break down food waste in your kitchen. If you have a septic system, however, check with local codes to see if disposals are permitted. In the past, there have been concerns about the environmental impact of these electric garbage guzzlers. Choices include continuous-feed disposals, which are operated by a wall or air switch and should be run only with a steady flow of water. The less common batch-feed disposal is activated when its lid is locked in place—a valuable safety feature, especially if you have young, curious children.

right • Two centuries blend together beautifully in this traditional-style kitchen. Although the sink is reminiscent of a vintage apron-front version from the early 19th century, the double-bowl design conveys 21st-century appeal with its sleek brushed-metal finish.

facing page • In this compact kitchen, a small stainless sink works beautifully with the other stainless components. A high faucet and hot water dispenser allow the most efficiency when working with large pots and pans.

Sink Materials

Sinks are available today in a wide range of materials from natural stone to glistening stainless steel. Choosing the right material depends on your personal taste, the style of your kitchen, and how the fixture pairs with your countertop. Besides being aesthetically pleasing, though, a kitchen sink also should be practical. Look for fixtures that offer a wide, deep bowl; solid construction; and a finish that's easy to clean.

STAINLESS STEEL

$–$$$

- Hygienic, durable, and long lasting.
- Easy to clean.
- Available in a range of finishes from brushed metal to polished; highly polished finishes show scratches.
- The thicker the material (the lower the gauge number), the quieter the sink.

CERAMIC

$$–$$$

- Available in a variety of colors.
- Can be hand painted or designed with decorative moldings.
- Offers a period look.
- Can scratch and chip.

PORCELAIN ENAMEL

$$

- Available in a range of colors.
- Can be ordered with or without an apron.
- Conveys a traditional look.
- Can scratch and chip.

STONE

$$$

- Available in granite and soapstone.
- Strong and durable, although soapstone can chip.
- Can blend visually with stone countertops.
- Must be sealed periodically.

PORCELAIN ENAMEL

STONE

CERAMIC

STAINLESS STEEL

PORCELAIN ENAMEL OVER CAST STEEL OR CAST IRON

Essentially made of white or colored glass that has been bonded to a molded metal shell at extreme temperatures, a porcelain enamel sink is manufactured in the same manner as classic claw-foot bathtubs. And the result is equally iconic. A white apron sink, which has a front lip that hangs down over the cabinet face, harkens back to the free-standing legged sinks in turn-of-the-20th-century farmhouse kitchens. But enameled sinks are generally installed with a sink base, not legs, and are available in a wide range of colors, either with or without the apron. The porcelain enamel finish, however, can scratch and chip over time.

CERAMIC

Sinks made from fireclay or vitreous china are longtime bathroom standards. They're relative newcomers to the kitchen, although they've quickly overtaken porcelain in popularity. Molded from clay and fired at extremely high temperatures, these units are often chosen for their decorative molded details and appealing glazes. Fine, sometimes hand-painted designs offer a highly ornamental look, which can sometimes be complemented by matching backsplash tiles, cabinet pulls, or other kitchen details. Like porcelain sinks, china units often have aprons — and are at slight risk for scratching and chipping.

facing page • A small space is used wisely. Cabinetry, countertops, appliances, and an ample farmhouse-style apron sink are situated within easy reach of one another. The bank of windows offers a much-needed visual respite while the homeowner performs tedious kitchen tasks.

above • Sinks that blend seamlessly with countertops make cleanup a pleasure. Here, an integral solid-surface, double-bowl sink is flush with a solid-surface countertop. This design allows the owner to wipe crumbs and puddles of water into the sink in one simple sweep.

DETAILS THAT WORK

A Clever Corner Shelf

In most homes, the only available space behind the kitchen sink is a shallow windowsill. Often this narrow ledge is altogether inadequate, especially when you consider the bottles of dishwashing liquid, trays of hand soap, and decorative items that collect here. To reduce overcrowding, the owner of this kitchen commissioned a deep corner shelf and topped it with granite to coordinate with the countertops.

SOLID SURFACE

Solid-surface sinks are made from various formulations of acrylic, which is high-grade plastic that's poured into a mold while it's in a molten state. The resulting bowl can be virtually any shape, is scratch resistant, and is available in a rainbow of colors. The sink can even be molded as one piece and bonded to the countertop, for an integral product that has no visible seams anywhere. And some manufacturers mix stone particles into the acrylic to produce sinks and countertops that offer a faux stone look. Another benefit of a solid-surface sink: If it does get scratched or nicked, the problem can be repaired by sanding it out.

STONE

Fabricated from slabs of stone that are glued together with strong epoxies, stone sinks are stunning to look at, and they're plenty strong and durable. They're almost always undermounted and often have apron fronts. Typically made from granite or soapstone, they're most often paired with matching stone countertops but can also be combined with any other countertop material. Hard stones like granite are extremely scratch resistant, whereas soapstone and other softer materials are susceptible to scratching and chipping and should be looked at as "living finishes," which means that a bit of wear and tear only adds to their charm. Honed stones have matte finishes that are easier to keep clean and smudge-free than polished finishes. And all stone sinks need to be regularly brushed with a sealer to protect them.

BRASS, COPPER, AND TITANIUM

Showy metals are reflective and colorful, but because they are susceptible to scratching and denting—and because they can tarnish and show water stains—they're best for low-use, high-visibility sinks, such as in wet bars.

above · A granite sink maintains a consistency in the countertop.

top left · A large double-bowl sink with a pull-out faucet right in the center has both good looks and great ergonomic design. Whether it's meal prep or cleanup, this duo maximizes efficiency.

left · An L-shaped faucet in brushed metal echoes the metal drying rack above the concrete counter, the nearby wall ovens, and towel bar–style pulls on the maple cabinetry.

facing page · An elegant vintage-style gooseneck bridge faucet, paired with a matching brushed-nickel side sprayer, is the perfect accompaniment for a single-bowl sink. This faucet can also be used with double-bowl sinks when both bowls are the same size.

Reflective Surfaces Enlarge a Small Kitchen

This narrow galley kitchen in a Boston apartment had no windows—only a door at each end. The owners wanted their new kitchen to be bright and to appear spacious. They also knew they wanted durable materials that would be easy to care for.

The careful use of reflective materials (even though some of them are quite dark) allows the room to be a well-lit space that's pleasant to work in. Unlike many kitchen designs that use light-colored cabinetry and dark stone countertops, here we see the opposite. The designer chose high-gloss laminate cabinetry in a rich brown shade with towel bar stainless-steel handles. The result: work areas that reflect light, especially around the sink and prep-area countertops.

The sliding glass–door wall cabinets above the sink add to the effect. The glass reflects light onto the sink, creating the illusion of having a window just above. Finally, the easy-care stainless-steel appliances were also chosen for their ability to reflect light.

left · Stainless-steel appliances, light-colored stone counters, and glossy laminate cabinetry in a rich brown reflect light into this narrow space, making it seem more spacious than it really is. By installing the gleaming stainless refrigerator near the door, additional light is cast into the space.

right · Further adding to the bright, open feel of the room is the limestone flooring. Like the limestone counters, the surface of the floor reflects light back into the space. Large tile set in a horizontal pattern make the room appear larger, too.

facing page · Frosted glass doors visually break up the long run of dark cabinetry and add texture to the room. In addition, they help create a feeling of openness since light both penetrates and bounces off their surface.

Faucets

Although you can get a faucet for less than $100, you'll be shortchanging yourself and your kitchen. For a bit more of an investment, you can choose from among a wide range of faucets that offer stylish good looks and convenience in one package.

FAUCET STYLE

Once upon a time, you could choose either a faucet with all of the latest conveniences or one with traditional styling, but now you can get a super-convenient faucet in any design you want, from state-of-the-art modern to retro cool. The most traditional look is still a faucet with two handles, of course, but that means a lot of fiddling around to get the water temperature just right. Luckily, these days there are vintage-style single-lever faucets, which put all of that fine tuning at the fingertips of one hand. Same goes for pull-out sprayers, which are now available on just about any style of faucet, even a gooseneck with Victorian detailing. And, of course, all of these options can also be found on units with sleek, contemporary styling.

above • Stainless details—from the faucet and sink to the ventilation hood, wine cooler, and knobs—don't detract from the beautiful bookmatched veneer cabinetry.

far left • In this kitchen, a small stainless-steel undermount sink with a pull-out spray faucet was added to the island. The set up allows family members to grab a glass of water or water plants when the main sink is being used.

left • Sometimes a mix of styles can provide both convenience and good looks. Here, a professional sprayer, just like the ones found in restaurant kitchens, works well with a more traditional gooseneck faucet.

facing page • A simple but elegant single-hole polished nickel gooseneck faucet has an artistic quality about it. Alongside this faucet is an air switch built into the countertop that operates the garbage disposal below the sink.

MOUNTING

Depending on how the faucet is mounted, your choice will have an effect on everything from your sink to your countertop to your backsplash. Some faucets need only a single hole in the sink—or in the countertop for undermount sinks. Others need three holes, sometimes with very specific spacing; and some don't get mounted in _____ sink or countertop but in the backspla_____ _____ to shop for your sink, countert_____ _____ backsplash, too, depending on _____ all at the same time—and fro_____ dealer, if possible.

MATERIALS

The innards of quality fau_____ solid brass or a brass comb_____ Ceramic disk valves are t_____ no rubber washers to wea_____ able mechanism is gene_____ warranty. And then ther_____ a matter of taste. You can get colo_____ course, and your choices of metals include chrome, brass, pewter, oil-rubbed bronze, or nickel. If you're selecting a metal, consider a "brushed" or "satin" product, which gives a matte finish that's less likely to show fingerprints or water marks. If you're going for a vintage look, though, polished nickel and oil-rubbed bronze are the more authentic choices.

facing page top · This single-lever faucet with a pull-out spray head seems to be taking a bow. The arc shape of the faucet mimics the swirl of the range hood, the curve of the countertop, and the round sink.

facing page middle · This faucet is a 100-year-old design, proof of its enduring style. It works beautifully with traditional or more contemporary sinks.

facing page bottom · An oil-rubbed bronze bridge faucet is paired with a lace-front, undermounted, fireclay apron sink. The design of the sink reflects the late-19th-century European revival of Oriental motifs in architecture. Because both fixtures are vintage in style they team up beautifully.

A single-lever faucet with pullout spray head complements this undermount stone sink. It's brushed-nickel finish mimics the soft finish of the soapstone sink and mixes well with the specks of gray in the polished granite countertop.

Pot Fillers

To paraphrase a 500-year-old saying, why bring pots of water to the stove when you can bring the stove to water? That's the idea behind the pot filler, a swing-arm faucet that gets installed in the backsplash behind the stove so you can fill your pots while they sit on a back burner. The pot filler folds flat against the backsplash when not in use and then swings out over your pot when you want water for cooking. Because it involves only a cold water feed, with no drain, the installation costs are minimal. Even if you're not doing a gut renovation, the plumbing lines can be installed in the space between the countertop and upper cabinets and, therefore, will be covered by the new backsplash.

top • The pot filler is all but hidden amid the tile work of the backsplash. Pot fillers mean no more lugging heavy pots from sink to stovetop.

above • Because this sink is extra deep, a pull-out drawer has extra-deep storage compartments. The integrated drain board in this sink eliminates the need for a plastic version on the countertop and is very attractive when not in use.

left • This pot filler, located by the right rear burner, features a heat-resistant handle, or valve, that stays cool to the touch even when positioned over a pot of boiling liquid.

facing page • To make the most out of the available floor space, the designer equipped this center island with hardworking and efficient features, including a second dishwasher, a prep sink, a built-in chopping block, and ample storage space.

FLOORS

From wood to stone to concrete, the choices for kitchen flooring

are more numerous than ever. In addition to the look,

you'll want to consider the material's moisture resistance,

durability, and comfort under foot.

Floor Materials

No floor in your house will take as much abuse as the one in your kitchen. Spills and drips are everyday occurrences here—and we're not talking about just water but also grape jelly and hot coffee and maple syrup. What's more, objects such as silverware and heavy pans will occasionally smash against the surface. And since the kitchen is the heart of the home, it'll also face lots of foot traffic from the whole family—as well as pets' paws and the "feet" of kitchen chairs sliding back from the table.

That's why durability and moisture resistance are must-haves for a kitchen floor and why, not so long ago, almost everyone installed either a resilient flooring material such as linoleum or a hard ceramic tile. But there are other issues to consider. For example, because you'll be standing for hours on this material, you might want something that offers a little give under foot. And if you have an open floor plan that links the kitchen to a family room or other living area, you may want a floor that can be used comfortably throughout the entire space or that will blend well with a different material that's used in the adjacent living area. Plus, a kitchen floor should harmonize with the textures and colors of the cabinets, countertops, and backsplash.

right• The fanciful print on this vinyl flooring adds pattern and interest to a space made up of neutral colors. Had the flooring been a solid color, the room would have taken on a cooler, more contemporary feel.

facing page top • This casual kitchen is enhanced by the diagonal pattern on the floor. The colors are striking against the white cabinetry.

facing page bottom • A light wood floor helps to keep a room bright. This one is outlined with a strip of mahogany, focusing the eye on the center of the room.

WOOD

Nearly everyone prefers hardwood floors for their living rooms, dining rooms, and the other public spaces of the home, so why not use it in the kitchen too? After all, wood offers a rich, warm look and provides a relatively forgiving surface on which to stand while you're preparing dinner. And today's hard polyurethane finishes will stand up well to the rigors of the kitchen. Best of all, there's a good chance that you already have wood flooring in your kitchen—it's just buried under layers of other floor coverings. Strip away those materials and perhaps all your floor needs is sanding and refinishing.

If you're installing new wood flooring, hardwoods such as red oak, maple, birch, and Brazilian cherry make hard-wearing surfaces. Softwoods such as pine and fir will show scratches, dents, dings, and other signs of wear (which, to some people, only add to their beauty). Wood flooring comes in 2¼-in. strips, wide planks, and tiles. And you'll get the toughest surface by choosing a factory-finished product. In the factory, manufacturers typically bake-on about seven coats of super-durable aluminum oxide sealant, a product that's far harder and longer-lasting than anything that's available for on-site application. What's more, choosing a factory finish means there's none of the mess of sanding and sealing the floor after it's installed. (Most factory-finished floors, however, have "eased" edges, which means there's a small V-groove between the boards to help disguise minor unevenness that occurs because they're not sanded flush after installation.)

above • Solid wood flooring goes with any style kitchen from contemporary to traditional. The same flooring continues into the dining room, but the saddle in the doorway helps delineate the transition.

left • By laying reclaimed pine flooring horizontally rather than vertically, the homeowners were able to accentuate the length of the room. The result is a kitchen that appears spacious and airy.

facing page • Chestnut-stained wide-plank rustic oak flooring was chosen for this renovated kitchen. It provides contrast to the warm painted cabinetry, accents the dark cherry island and provides a comfortable surface to stand and work on. Todays' high-quality finishes make wood floors a very practical and beautiful flooring choice.

Another option is engineered wood, which is made from plywood with a solid "wear layer" on top. These floors are ideal for installation over concrete and below grade because they're not subject to cupping and swelling from moisture as solid wood is. Plus, they're what's known as "floating floors," which means that they don't get fastened to the subfloor at all, so any shifts caused by changing moisture conditions won't result in damage. But engineered flooring can be sanded and refinished only once or twice as opposed to the six or seven sandings that most standard wood flooring can take. Engineered flooring is usually, but not always, factory finished, however, so the initial surface should last for a long time.

facing page • This home's original wide plank fir floor was uncovered during renovation to provide a warm, natural feel to this space.

above • Looking for a "green" floor? Environmentally friendly bamboo is grown on plantations and replenishes itself very quickly after harvest. Bamboo is a hard, durable surface for use in any room, especially the kitchen.

below • Tile floors are very durable and can provide a variety of colors and patterns. This one complements the rich cherry cabinetry and granite countertops in the same tone.

DETAILS THAT WORK

Inlay Flooring

Although red oak strip flooring provides an already impressive contrast to the white cabinetry in this kitchen, the owners went one step further. They commissioned a border of narrow inlaid strips of ebony on the floor around the cabinetry. The treatment adds emphasis to the cabinets and draws attention to the rich red oak.

TILE

Unlike wood, tile is impervious to the two major scourges of kitchen floors: water and foot traffic. Ceramic, porcelain, and stone tiles that are rated for kitchen flooring use—based on their scratch resistance and porosity (which a good retailer can tell you about)—are essentially immune to spills and drops. What's more, the nearly endless choices of colors, textures, and patterns that you can create with tile make this flooring a wonderful medium for creative expression. You can choose anything from a large handmade terra cotta tile with a Southwestern flair to a mosaic of tiny porcelain hexagons that have a Victorian look to an elegant Italian limestone that brings natural beauty into your home.

Be aware, though, that polished stones and shiny ceramic glazes can leave the floor slippery when wet, so you'll be better off choosing a honed stone finish or ceramic tile that's either textured or unglazed. Also, some ceramic tiles and all stone tiles require frequent sealing to prevent them from absorbing stains or, in the case of limestone and marble, from disintegrating as a result of contact with acidic foods such as fruit juices and wine. And unless you use an epoxy grout, you'll definitely want to seal your grout to prevent it from darkening and staining over time. Remember too that almost anything that falls onto a tile floor is likely to break. Finally, standing on a hard tile floor for hours on end can be very tiring, so think about a cushy throw rug or a sturdy stool with a seat at the right height for working at your countertops.

left • Small tiles positioned as diamonds provide a colorful accent in this kitchen. This kind of treatment works well in large spaces since the spots of color call attention to the floor.

above • This neutral-tone tile floor would blend with any color scheme. A mottled finish such as this is a maintenance dream because it disguises dirt and debris—you won't be running for the broom with every dropped crumb.

below • Large 12-in. tiles placed on the diagonal add visual interest. The soft grey muted tones complement the blue countertops without competing with them for attention.

A variety of sizes and color tones give this tile floor a sense of antiquity. It is an ideal complement to the Old World—style cabinetry in this kitchen.

Tile Makes a Small Space Feel Larger

The biggest challenge of this kitchen renovation in a cottage on the Maine coast was to open up the space and make the narrow room seem wider. The 7-ft.-wide room is situated in what was originally a porch.

The bold colors and strong pattern of the floor tile demand attention and make the floor area appear larger than it is. Using a geometric pattern on the floor emphasizes the length of the room and minimizes the focus on the room's lack of width. The floor's pattern is based on one of the homeowner's quilts; laying the individual tiles was laborious, but it was well worth the effort.

Other elements that visually expand the space include windows on both outside walls that not only take advantage of the views but also draw the eye beyond the room. Glass doors in the wall cabinets increases the illusion of depth in the space, and the glass reflects the natural light from the windows.

The base cabinets on the inside walls opposite the sink are only 12 in. deep, which allows for a wide enough aisle between the two banks of cabinetry. The vaulted ceiling and the pass-through window to the living room also add to the overall spacious feeling of this otherwise small kitchen.

left • By using 12-in.-deep base cabinets on the inside wall, the designer was able to achieve maximum storage and functionality while creating a reasonable 42-in.-wide aisle.

facing page • The geometric pattern of the tile floor captures the eye and draws it down the length of the room rather than concentrating it on the aisle's narrow width. The windows at the end of the space visually extend the area even further.

below • An interior window, which opens into the family room with its fireplace, adds another view from the narrow kitchen, adding to its feeling of spaciousness.

RESILIENT MATERIALS

Made from vinyl, polyurethane, rubber, or linoleum, manufactured flooring comes in a wide range of colors, patterns, and textures. Because resilient materials are very thin, you can often lay them on top of an existing floor without raising it much higher than the adjacent floors. Some materials have faux stone or tile looks, others take on the pixilated appearance of abstract art, and still others come in retro 1950s diner styles.

Resilient floors are typically available in sheets that are 12 ft. wide, which means you may not need any seams in your kitchen floor. That makes for a very waterproof floor, although the materials are generally fairly soft and susceptible to denting and tearing. Resilient materials are also available in 12-in. by 12-in. tiles, which allow you to mix and match shapes and colors. Tiles are far simpler for a do-it-yourselfer to install than sheet goods, but the floor's numerous seams mean that spills have the potential to find their way to the subfloor.

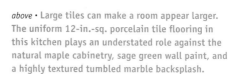

above • Large tiles can make a room appear larger. The uniform 12-in.-sq. porcelain tile flooring in this kitchen plays an understated role against the natural maple cabinetry, sage green wall paint, and a highly textured tumbled marble backsplash.

left • Sheet vinyl in a blue and yellow geometric pattern adds necessary visual appeal to this kitchen with its all-white cabinets. The tiled backsplash and a blue plaid window treatment do their part to enliven the space.

right • Green wall paint in this butler's pantry and adjoining kitchen is accented by the random diamond pattern in the linoleum floor. The diamond shape, which appears to be leading traffic into the kitchen, visually connects the two spaces.

facing page • Cork is naturally beautiful and, like linoleum and vinyl, is extremely comfortable to stand on. It's especially popular with those who are looking for "green" design since it comes from a renewable natural resource.

Environmentally Friendly Cork and Bamboo

Not only do cork and bamboo bring wonderful hues and complex textures to the kitchen floor but they're environmentally friendly. Cork is made from the bark of a Mediterranean oak tree, which regenerates every 10 years or so; and bamboo is made from an Asian grass, which matures in about 6 years. Thus these products are much more renewable than wood, which requires many decades to reach harvestable size.

Cork is typically sold as a tile or sheet that's very easy to install, and because it contains millions of air pockets within its cells, it's extremely soft and warm underfoot and makes excellent sound proofing as well. It needs to be sealed to protect it from moisture—though it's often sealed in the factory. Bamboo is more like wood in terms of hardness and feel, and it typically comes "natural," which is a light color, or "caramelized," which results in a mellow brown that is created when the manufacturer heats the bamboo, caramelizing the sugars in its fibers. It, too, needs sealing, typically with polyurethane and usually on site.

Flooring

When ███████████████████████████
After a█████████████████████████
kitchen████████████████████████
mind b███████████████████████
than ot██████████████████████
nance.███████████████████████
you ha███████████████████████
saying ███████████████████████
ultimately complement the design of your kitchen.

VINYL
$

- Resilient, so it's relatively soft underfoot.
- Easy to install and maintain.
- Available in a variety of colors and patterns as well as in sheet and tile form.
- High-quality vinyl is durable, handsome, and colorfast; lower cost vinyl can yellow or lose its pattern over time.
- Sheet vinyl is more resistant to water than vinyl tile because it has fewer seams.

BAMBOO
$$$

- Like wood, provides warmth and natural beauty.
- Can be stained with certain dye-based stains.
- Very durable; harder than oak.
- Can be refinished numerous times.

WOOD
$$$

- Warm color and exposed grain offer natural beauty.
- Resilient underfoot.
- Solid wood expands and contracts with changes in humidity, leaving gaps.
- Soft woods such as pine will dent and scratch easier than hardwoods like oak.
- Can be refinished; engineered wood can be refinished only a limited number of times.

TILE
$$

- Broad assortment of colors and textures.
- Extremely durable and long lasting.
- Hard underfoot; can be uncomfortable if standing for long periods of time.
- Must be sealed to resist stains.
- Grout requires periodic sealing.

CONCRETE

STONE

STONE
$$$

- Natural material with unrivaled beauty.
- Like tile, durable and long lasting.
- Polished stone as opposed to a honed finish can leave floors slippery when wet.
- Nonresilient; to improve comfort, use accent rugs.
- Requires periodic sealing against stains and moisture.

LAMINATE
$$

- Wide array of colors and pattern options, including stone, wood, and tile designs.
- Easy to maintain.
- High-quality laminate will resist dents, scratches, and water damage.
- Can be purchased in snap-down form.
- Relatively comfortable to stand on.

LINOLEUM
$$

- A natural product made from linseed oil and a mix of materials such as cork, wood, and limestone.
- Available in multiple attractive colors in sheet, tile, and snap-down forms.
- Comfortable underfoot.
- New no-wax surfaces make it easy to maintain.
- Durable and quiet.

CORK
$$

- An environmentally sustainable material.
- Provides extreme comfort underfoot.
- Can be purchased in plank form or as solid tiles.
- Natural thermal insulation reduces noise.
- Not resistant to fading or denting.

CONCRETE
$$$

- Extremely durable and long lasting.
- Can be tinted in a variety of colors.
- Patterns and textures can be imprinted easily.
- Nonresilient; can be uncomfortable if standing for long periods of time.
- Must be sealed against staining.

VINYL

WOOD

TILE

CONCRETE

Poured in place, tinted to any color of the rainbow, and polished smooth, concrete makes for a floor that's beautiful, durable, and unique. It's also oblivious to any spill, drop, or tracked-in dirt; but any glassware or dinnerware that falls on it is going to break. Concrete isn't for everyone, though, because it's porous and needs regular sealing so that it won't stain and because it's very hard and cold on bare feet. Consider warming the floor with radiant heat, using throw rugs, and sitting on a stool while working at the counter.

Radiant Floor Heat

Radiant floor heat is an ideal way to heat your kitchen—especially if you've got a tile, stone, concrete, or wood floor, which can be chilly to bare feet on cold mornings. Installed under any type of flooring material, radiant heat systems are made up of a series of ducts in which water circulates. As the water warms up, heat radiates through the flooring and into the room. Unlike forced hot air or hot-water baseboard heat which can cause drafts, radiant heat is energy-efficient. It's also hidden from view, eliminating the need for registers and baseboards.

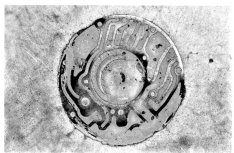

above· When installing a concrete floor, add personality by inlaying details. If the inlays will be raised so they're not even with the floor be sure to position them where they can be admired but not tripped over.

left · The countertop, flooring, and island are all of the same durable material, stained concrete. The understated neutral color of the concrete allows the natural maple cabinetry to take center stage and for the handmade copper hood to be the focal point of the room.

The concrete floor in this California kitchen was divided by transecting cuts. When stained, the concrete takes on a slightly aged appearance.

LAMINATE

Made to look like anything from Brazilian cherry to slate, laminate floors are actually fiberboard planks topped with photographic images of the real thing and coated with clear plastic "wear layers." Laminates are easy for do-it-yourselfers to install because they're floating floors; you simply snap them together at their edges and don't fasten them to the subfloor at all. That also means you can use them directly over a concrete slab as well as below grade because any movement caused by moisture won't damage the floor.

Laminates can offer a good approximation of the look of wood or stone for less cost. Just make sure to choose a product with a number of different photographic images of the stone or wood or tile that the floor is imitating—instead of only a single image that repeats on every piece of laminate—so the effect will appear more natural. Laminates that are embossed with the texture of wood grain or honed stone (or whatever the photographs show) fool the eye even more.

Try to keep tracked-in grit off your laminate floor, because it can scratch the wear layer. And avoid getting the floors too wet (dry mopping is best) because moisture can work into the seams between the planks, causing them to separate slightly, creating telltale signs that the floor is made from laminate and not real wood or tile.

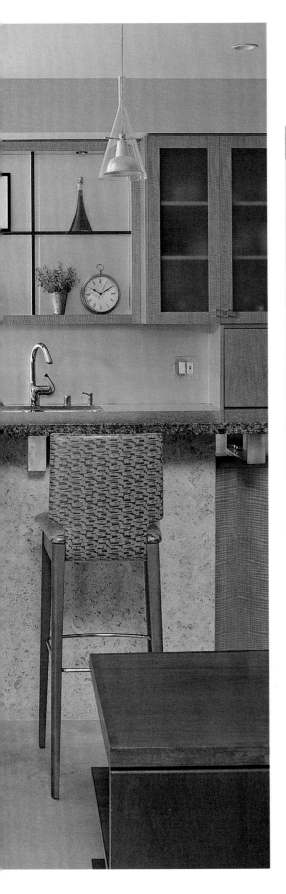

Combining Materials

Using two or more kinds of flooring materials can help delineate activity areas within a space. Here, wood flooring in the kitchen area gets protection from the grit, grime, and moisture tracked in from the outside. The narrow tile path clearly defines a separate area, making it clear to guests and visitors that mudroom and outdoor traffic should follow a clear course and stay off of the wood floor.

left • Some granites are not only available for countertop use but also in 12-in.-sq. floor tiles, allowing for a perfect match.

facing page • A concrete floor can be stained and polished to provide a durable, low-maintenance flooring choice. Concrete can blend with just about any style from rustic to contemporary.

far left facing page • The tile floor in this contemporary kitchen is rich in texture and pattern. It makes a stark contrast to the white laminate cabinetry. Wedding the two elements together are cabinet pulls in an earthy copper color, a shade that appears in the flooring.

APPLIANCES

Like trading up to a new car, getting new appliances means

a serious upgrade in convenience, style, and features. And today's refrigerators,

ranges, and dishwashers all come in a wide variety of appealing designs.

To See or Not to See?

Your appliances can be the focal points of your kitchen or they can virtually disappear into the background. It's up to you. The gleaming surfaces of professional-style equipment can serve as the centerpieces for an entire kitchen design, with all of the other elements providing the setting for these jewels. Or you can choose appliances that are built into your cabinetry and concealed behind paneled door fronts. There's plenty of middle ground too, with numerous appliances that are neither flashy nor concealed.

above • This kitchen packs a lot—including a TV—into a small space. The position of the refrigerator is perfect; it's easy for family and guests lounging on the patio to step just inside the sliding door and grab a snack or beverage.

left • If not for the architectural prominence given to the cooking area, the cooktop would almost disappear into the countertop. Keeping the appliances in the same black and stainless color family allows the blue cabinetry to be the primary focus.

facing page • Although stainless steel is a popular finish for ranges, there are other options available. Here, a black professional-style range mixes in well with the black soapstone countertops and sink. Adding further appeal to this vintage-style kitchen is pine cabinetry with furniture details and the brick floor.

DETAILS THAT WORK

Appliance Shelves

If you don't have adequate counter space, or even if you do and simply want to keep it free of clutter, consider installing appliance shelves. A shelf such as this one pops up and out of base cabinetry with ease, eliminating the need to lift heavy items and providing a steady surface for electric mixers or food processors.

Cooling Tools

Remember when the automatic ice maker seemed like a cutting-edge freezer option? Well, these days *filtered* water and ice dispensers are practically standard features—as are a host of other useful innovations, from automated defrosters to drawers with their own temperature controls, door trays that hold gallon jugs of milk, and leakproof glass shelving. But choosing the features you want is actually the easy part of buying a refrigerator. The bigger challenge is deciding on the kind of package you want all of that convenience to come in, and that means choosing between three basic refrigerator types.

above • Installing refrigerator or freezer drawers next to a prep sink or in an island puts extra storage where you need it most. This refrigerator drawer is conveniently positioned directly across from the center island.

facing page • Because it's set away from the rest of the work triangle, the refrigerator is seemingly its own little work area, complete with adjacent countertop, storage cabinets above and at the side, and recessed ceiling light.

left • Most of the appliances are hidden in this kitchen thanks to a design feature called full integration. By design, this refrigerator accepts full-size panels that integrate the appliance with surrounding cabinetry. Full integration also means the appliance accepts cabinet hardware that matches your other cabinetry hardware.

FREESTANDING

This is probably what you think of when you picture a refrigerator: a standalone appliance that simply gets connected to a power source (and probably a water supply) and then wheeled into an open spot within a wall of cabinets. Most freestanding units are 27 in. to 32 in. deep, which means that they protrude beyond the 24-in.-deep base cabinets (although you can get cabinet-depth models). Freestanding refrigerators are by far the most common choice, but they can look extraordinary: Choose a sleek stainless-steel model or one with a rich retro-colored enamel finish, and it will make a strong design statement.

above • Although refrigerators with side-by-side doors were most popular in the 1980s and 1990s, this example doesn't look dated. Its stainless surface adds texture and interest to the space and harmonizes with the adjacent stainless-steel sink and counter.

right • An ultra-contemporary kitchen calls for appliances with the same feeling. Not only does the stainless steel mix well with the frosted glass cabinet doors, but even the hardware on the cabinetry and refrigerator complement the overall design.

Refrigerator Door Configurations

Multiple Freezer Drawers

These provide a little more freezer storage than their single-drawer refrigerator/freezer counterparts. They can be fully integrated with cabinetry to take on the appearance of a pantry cabinet.

Freezer on the Bottom

This is generally considered the best option because it places the often-used refrigerator compartment at eye level. Full-width shelves in both sections make it easy to store large dishes and specialty items.

Armorie or French-Style Door

This style provides all the features and advantages of a traditional freezer on the bottom with the added benefit of split doors. It's ideal for smaller kitchens where aisle width may be less than optimum.

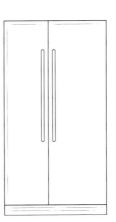

Freezer on the Top

This is the standard configuration of refrigerator/freezer units and is the least expensive style. However, most refrigerated items are below eye level. Deep, wide shelves in both compartments allow storage of a variety of items.

Side by Side

The traditional style is a great option for small spaces but does not provide full-width shelves in either compartment. Because the doors are relatively small, they do not intrude into walkways and aisles. French door or armoire-style units give you the storage capacity of full-width shelves with the convenience of smaller doors.

BUILT-INS

Built-in refrigerators are installed in the cabinetry, in much the same manner as dishwashers, so only the doors are visible. And often, those doors are treated with panels that match the cabinet doors, so the machine quite literally blends into the woodwork. Alternatively, the doors can be left unpaneled so the appliance is easily recognized for what it is. Built-in refrigerators are only 24 in. deep to sit flush with the cabinets. That provides easy access to foodstuffs that migrate to the rear but limits capacity, so you may want to choose one that's a few inches wider than your old freestanding unit.

above • The king of all residential refrigerators, this 48-in.-wide model includes a glass door with refrigerator and freezer drawers. If your budget allows, this professional-looking unit will fill the bill and then some.

left • Because all the major appliances are positioned along one side of this kitchen, their finish makes a strong statement. The decidedly contemporary design of the gleaming appliances contrasts well with the prairie-style cabinetry, subway tile backsplash, and dark-stained oak floors.

facing page • In keeping with the farmhouse character of this space, the refrigerator is covered with beaded-board wainscot that matches the surrounding cabinetry.

UNDERCOUNTER

Though they're short enough to fit under a standard countertop, diminutive, undercounter chillers are nothing like those mini-refrigerators from your college dorm days. Indeed, these machines are the height of high-end kitchen style. They're designed to be used in addition to a main refrigerator, and they're generally available in the same styles as their full-size cousins. There are three main types of undercounter refrigerators:

- *Wine chillers* keep your favorite bottles on their sides (so the corks stay fresh) and at optimal storing (and sipping) temperature—and they often have multiple temperature zones for handling different types of vintages. They are commonly installed in wet bars but are found in many kitchens as well.

- *Modular drawer refrigerators* put their cooling power into large cabinet drawers and can have fronts that match the rest of the cabinets. They're convenient for storing different types of foodstuffs in various locations around the kitchen. You might, for example, place a drawer in a convenient spot where guests can help themselves to cold drinks during parties or locate one near the prep sink for storing fruits and vegetables.

- *Full-door undercounter models* are another alternative for stocking a beverage center or just adding extra capacity to the kitchen. You can select one that matches the main appliance or install a door panel so it blends in with the cabinets. They cost about half the price of modular drawer units and are available as refrigerator only, freezer only, or dual compartment.

Wine Coolers

Whether you're a wine enthusiast or just an occasional wine-with-dinner type, you may want a dedicated wine cooler in your kitchen. Tall built-in wine coolers hold hundreds of bottles, whereas their under-the-counter counterparts hold up to 60 bottles. Features to look for include dual cooling zones for reds and whites, pull-out shelves that reduce stooping and reaching, and door locks. Some models have glass doors, and others have solid panels that can be finished to match your cabinetry.

top · A custom built-in wine closet located off of the kitchen provides storage for wine while adding architectural interest. Two refrigerator drawers keep white wine at the proper temperature.

left · Wine coolers are finding their way into many kitchens. This 27-in.-wide, full-height cooler features a custom-stained glass door, allowing the unit to take center stage in this kitchen design.

facing page · A full-service buffet makes entertaining a breeze because everything guests need—chilled drinks and wine, serving dishes, and barware—is all in the same place.

Modern Appliances Meet Vintage Cabinetry

When the homeowners purchased this 1892 farmhouse in rural Utah, they knew immediately that the kitchen was in need of a complete overhaul. The original space consisted of nothing more than a stove and one cabinet. There was no refrigerator and no plumbing. Their aim was to include state-of-the-art appliances without sacrificing the homestead flavor of the home.

To accomplish this, they selected custom cabinets with a period look and appliances that were specially designed to accept cabinetry fronts. The new refrigerator resembles a vintage pantry, and the dishwasher looks like a four-drawer base cabinet. The bun feet on all the base cabinets further add to the furniture feel of the kitchen. Integrating the appliances within the cabinetry makes you think there are no modern conveniences in the room.

Gray granite countertops and a black fireclay farmhouse apron sink play off the black wrought-iron hinges and handles and contrast with the classic white cabinetry. Enhancing the kitchen's period feel is the reclaimed antique fir flooring.

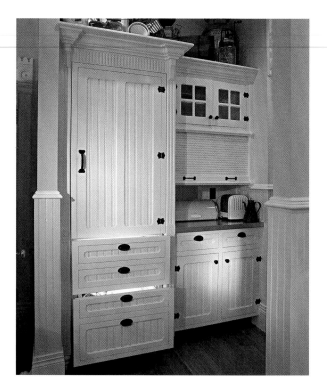

above • This fully integrated refrigerator with custom door-style panels is reminiscent of a vintage pantry.

left • When closed, this fully integrated dishwasher looks like a four-drawer base cabinet. When open, the controls are revealed.

facing page • The black fireclay farmhouse apron sink harmonizes with the black wrought-iron hinges and handles, contrasting well with the classic white cabinetry.

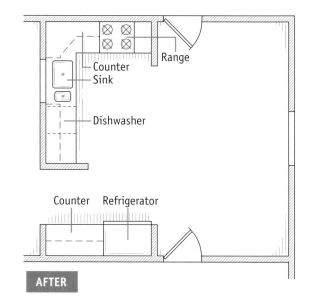

AFTER

Cooking Tools

Whether you'll be cooking with gas or electricity—or both, for that matter, because gas is generally considered best for the cooktop and electricity for the oven—you have several different formats to choose from for your appliances. Don't forget that other cooking machine, the microwave, which is the most frequently used oven in many homes.

above left • Positioning a cooktop or stove along a wall instead of in an island allows you the option of installing a pot filler behind it.

above right • If you prefer wood in your kitchen instead of stainless steel or other metals, create a showpiece like this custom hood in warm cherry. Chicken-wire door inserts on each side of the range, a mantle shelf, and a tile backsplash add delightful details.

left • An oversize appliance garage is an ideal way to store a microwave oven and keep it hidden when not in use. This type of storage offers an added benefit: Replacing the microwave is easy because it's not built in to the cabinetry.

facing page • Multilevels for multitasking. Gleaming stainless appliances—including double wall ovens, a microwave oven, and a warming drawer—open shelves, and glass mullion doors, add texture and interest to this space.

Ranges

When choosing a range, first decide what configuration you need. A cooktop is countertop mounted and equipped with up to eight burners or a combination of burners and other accessories such as a grill, griddle, deep-fryer, or even a built-in wok. Wall ovens are mounted in the cabinetry and can have a single or double oven, or a combination of oven and microwave or oven and convection oven. And finally, a range is a combination of cooktop and oven. Ranges can either slide into a space between cabinets or they can be freestanding. Consider also how much counter space you want to give up—an oven installed below a cooktop (in a base cabinet or range) or in a wall gives maximum space—and what type and how much cooking you really do. Eight burners and two giant ovens pump up the look of a kitchen, but how often will you have eight pots simmering and two ovens roasting all at once?

right • A professional-style range with two ovens becomes the focal point in this kitchen. The stainless steel harmonizes with the gray granite backsplash, while the cherry cabinets warm up the large space.

facing page • The location of this cooktop allows the chef to enjoy the activities going on in the family room area. The multiple windows provide welcome fresh air because there is no built-in ventilation.

COOKTOPS AND WALL OVEN(S)
$–$$$$

- Oven can be placed at a convenient height and cooktop can be installed in a variety of locations such as in the middle of an island.
- Style flexibility; choices include a convection and/or self-cleaning oven and a glass top, gas, or induction cooktop.
- Ability to have up to eight burners with one or two ovens.
- Cooktop requires a base cabinet; a wall oven needs either a tall cabinet or a base cabinet.
- If not located by the cooktop, oven may not be adequately served by ventilation.

SLIDE-IN AND FREESTANDING RANGES
$–$$$$

- Available in a range of styles from plain and modest to professional and high end.
- Do not require cabinetry to be fitted around them because they stand alone.
- Some models offer a gas cooktop with an electric oven.
- Not convenient in kitchens in which there is more than one cook.
- The oven is low to the floor.

FREESTANDING RANGE

Freestanding ranges are out in the open for all to see and appreciate. They can be standard four-burner, 30-in.-wide units or six- to eight-burner, oversize restaurant-style ranges that include griddles and warming trays. Antique stoves fit into this category as well. And as with refrigerators, ranges can be anything from plain and simple to extremely high style.

above • A white microwave oven and slide-in range provide a clean, crisp look in this kitchen. Black appliances would have created a more dramatic statement.

right • At first glance this range seems to be an antique, but it is actually a contemporary, state-of-the-art appliance. The freestanding model is simply hidden beneath a 1930s-style exterior, which adds a nostalgic look to the kitchen.

facing page • Many appliances are available in a variety of colors, but the old standbys are black and white. Using one of these two allows the other major components of the kitchen—cabinetry, countertops, backsplash, and floor—to add as much visual interest as desired.

Gas vs. Electric

It's an age-old kitchen debate: Should your cooking appliances use gas or electricity? In the past, electric burners were not as infinitely adjustable as gas-fired ones. And gas burners heated up more quickly but didn't clean up as well. With the advent of radiant cooktops, new electric burners heat quicker and have finer adjustments. And now many gas ovens have a self-cleaning feature. The best news yet? Many manufacturers now offer dual-fuel ranges that have gas burners and electric ovens.

COOKTOPS AND WALL OVENS

Rather than buying a range, you might consider two separate pieces of equipment: a cooktop and a wall oven (or ovens). The cooktop gets installed right in your countertop, and the wall oven is inserted into a cutout in the wall or into a tall and deep cabinet. This offers a fitted look that can downplay the visual importance of the cooking appliances, and it also has some practical advantages. For example, it means you can place your cooktop in almost any spot you want, such as in the middle of an island, and can have storage drawers for your pots and pans right underneath it. Also, it means you can place the oven at chest height (the bottom of the oven should be 36 in. high), which is the most convenient location for maneuvering dishes in and out. And it allows you to locate the hot oven away from the main cooking zone—and out of the reach of young children. And, if you want extra cooking capacity, double wall ovens can be easier to work into tight kitchen layouts than a wide range with two oven compartments.

above • When this kitchen was remodeled, a closet was converted to house a built-in oven and microwave.

right • Task lights built into this hood not only reflect the shiny surface of the cooktop but help the chef see when preparing dinner.

DETAILS THAT WORK

A Range of Hoods

In this western-style kitchen, the variety of cooking appliances required different ventilation systems. Over the double cooktops, the hood is high enough to allow the chef to stand at the counter. Over the wood-burning fireplace, which is used for cooking only occasionally, the hood is considerably lower so that it can safely capture the large volume of smoke from the burning wood.

above • Providing both entertainment and practicality, this fireplace lets wood-burning pizza lovers grill year-round, then sit by the fire to enjoy it.

A Thoughtful Layout

The white-painted cabinet and the worn linoleum floor weren't all that was wrong with this kitchen in a 1930s two-story California bungalow. The appliances were also badly outdated. The homeowners wanted to make the most of their limited space in the galley kitchen while honoring the historical architecture of their home.

When selecting the appliances, the goal was to buy high-quality products in a finish that would complement the new cherry cabinetry. The neutral color of the stainless steel does that, plus reflects light and provides a subtle texture.

Placement of the appliances was critical to the function of the kitchen. The cleanup sink, range, and refrigerator form a work triangle; there is also plenty of counter space between each appliance. Placing the microwave next to the refrigerator is good planning because most food that goes into the microwave comes directly from the refrigerator or freezer. The countertop under the microwave provides prep space.

On the opposite wall, the sink is next to the dishwasher, and the upper cabinets hold dishes and glassware. The result is an efficient workflow: Dirty dishes go from sink to dishwasher, and clean ones go right into the upper cabinet. The location of the glass-door wine cooler makes it easy to retrieve a favorite bottle, and its angled placement at the end of the run of cabinets eases the flow between the kitchen and the adjacent dining room.

right • Prairie-style glass cabinet doors add texture and an open and airy feeling to the space. The stainless-steel dishwasher and glass-door wine cooler augment the element of texture and help break up the long expanse of cabinetry.

facing page • The refrigerator, microwave, and range and hood are positioned to ensure adequate counter space for food prep.

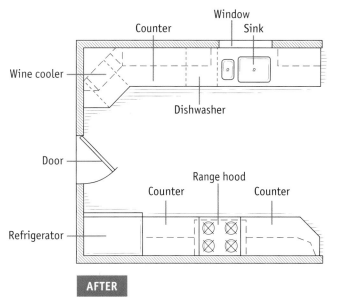

Window

Counter

Sink

Wine cooler

Dishwasher

Door

Range hood

Counter

Counter

Refrigerator

AFTER

WARMING DRAWERS

Warming drawers give you a convenient place to keep food warm and moist until you're ready to serve it; the units usually have variable temperature controls that go up to about 200°F. You can locate one below a built-in oven or in an extra-deep cabinet almost anywhere you want it, such as near a serving area or the access point to the dining room. Warming drawers can be finished to match the other appliances in your kitchen, or the drawer fronts can match your cabinetry

MICROWAVE OVENS

At first, microwaves were big boxes that ate up loads of counter space. Then they were combined with ventilation hoods and installed over the cooktop or range. But these days, there's another option: the built-in microwave. This unit is installed in the same manner as a wall oven and can be paired with an oven or used on its own. In either case, the microwave will be most convenient to operate if located at chest height, typically 48 in. to 54 in. from the floor.

Trash Compactors

Trash compactors can reduce the volume of rubbish you generate by using up to 5,000 lb. of pressure to compress upward of 17 regular bags of garbage into 1, albeit very heavy, bag. Some models come equipped with a charcoal filter or automatic deodorizing spray to eliminate smells. Other features to look for include a removable key to prevent accidental operation, a toe-bar drawer opener, noise insulation, and a tilt-away drawer to make it easy to remove the compacted bags.

above • A warming oven can be used in place of a second oven. If you decide to add one to your kitchen, be sure to locate it conveniently near your stove.

left • A hood in warm copper complements the dark-colored granite counter in this otherwise all-white space.

facing page • Stainless-steel appliances mix well with the gray granite countertops and backsplash in this kitchen. The built-in microwave oven blends evenly with the upper cabinets.

Hoods

There's a variety of hoods to complement every style of kitchen cabinetry from Mediterranean to modern. While some hoods are available prefinished in a variety of metals—stainless steel is the most popular—others are designed to be trimmed out with wood, tile, or even decorative plaster. Because hoods are subjected to grease and smoke, look for one that is easy to clean. Some have easy-to-remove, dishwasher-safe screens and filters. Also consider a hood's lighting options. Units with built-in task lighting, either fluorescent or halogen, keep you from cooking in the dark.

1. Looking more like a piece of art than a kitchen appliance, this hand-hammered, mottled copper hood is the focal point of the kitchen. **2.** Fitting right in among contemporary-style cabinetry is a sleek, stainless-steel hood. **3.** A copper rail for hanging pots and pans surrounds this ample brushed-metal island hood.

4

5

4. A custom ball-peen hammered copper hood takes center stage in this Arts and Crafts kitchen. 5. This futuristic-looking hood is right in style with the varied textures and colors in this kitchen.

Dishwashers

The big news about dishwashers is how quiet they've become. If you have an old unit, you probably have to crank up the volume on your television when the dishwasher is running in the next room. Some of the new machines are so silent that you can't even tell when they're operating. Plus they're much more efficient than the older equipment, using only a fraction of the water and electricity that their predecessors use. And they come in stylish designs that match the motif of your other appliances or can be covered with wood panels. There are even miniature units for installing under the kitchen sink or, like refrigerators and warming ovens, in large drawers. Some dishwashers have built-in garbage-disposal-like blades that automatically grind up debris. That makes them a bit noisier than other units, but you won't have to rinse the filter yourself, which is a requirement for the quietest machines.

above • Until you open the drawers, you might think storage cabinets were behind this paneling, not a dishwasher.

right • Still popular, the sleek black dishwasher works with just about any style of cabinetry. And because most stainless steel appliances have black accents, the black dishwasher will coordinate nicely if you decide to trade up other appliances.

facing page • This well-planned kitchen features two sinks, with the dishwasher rightly positioned in the cleanup area. The beefy-feeling stainless appliances and fixtures fit well with the openness of the space.

Energy-Efficient Appliances

Affixed to all appliances today is an energy guide sticker that shows the average annual energy costs of a particular model. You can now purchase dishwashers that use 4 gal. of water per load compared to other models that use up to 12 gal. Refrigerator designers have also made great progress in improving energy efficiency. Generally, models with a top-mounted freezer use the least electricity (side-by-side models use the most).

FINISHING

While your selections for paint, light fixtures, bar stools, and window treatments won't involve nearly as much money as some of the more permanent parts of the kitchen, they will still have a big effect on the look and feel of the space.

TOUCHES

Lighting

There was a time when most kitchens got their light from a big fluorescent fixture in the middle of the ceiling. It was so bright that it illuminated the whole room, but with a cold, antiseptic glow that strained the eyes. Today, there are much better lighting options—from hidden undercabinet systems that bathe the countertops with light to colorful glass pendants that hang over islands. A combination of these fixtures will light your room attractively, comfortably, and without shadows. Plus, many of the fixtures themselves will provide eye-catching design elements in their own rights. As you develop your lighting plan, think about three different kinds of lighting: general, task, and accent.

above • This kitchen is well lit with natural light via a skylight. But the lighting plan is also effective: undercabinet lights illuminate the backsplash area, hanging pendants provide task lighting at the breakfast bar, and recessed downlights provide both task and ambient lighting.

left • Fluorescent lights installed beneath the wall cabinets in this kitchen provide lighting for tasks such as referring to recipes and preparing meals. The stainless-steel backsplash does its part in brightening the space, too. The polished surface reflects light into the center of the room.

facing page • Chandeliers add a decorative element to this room and provide a key function: They wash light over the cooktop and breakfast bar for kitchen tasks. Two fixtures, as opposed to one or three, are ideal for this modestly sized granite-top island.

Energy-Efficient Lighting

The most significant advancement in residential lighting in recent years is the development of compact fluorescent lamps (CFLs). Unlike their larger predecessor, with its irritating flicker and eerie green hue, CFLs produce warm and inviting light similar to incandescent bulbs, but they last 10 to 15 times longer. That means less bulb changing. You can replace an incandescent lamp with a CFL that is roughly one-quarter to one-half of its wattage, which amounts to a 75 percent energy savings.

above • The three-lamp chandelier over the small island is big enough to provide ambient lighting for the whole kitchen. Lots of natural light from the windows over the sink help, too, as does the accent lighting in the dish cabinet.

above right • Accent lights are a perfect way to introduce fun and personality into any space since they're not designed to be the sole provider of light. The star pendant hanging from the blue ceiling is reminiscent of a nighttime sky.

right • Task lighting is important to help focus attention on the key work areas. This large range hood features built-in lights that provide ample light for the stove and surrounding countertop areas.

facing page • Uplights placed in the space between the wall cabinets and the ceiling in this room wash light over the perimeter of the ceiling. The effect adds a certain amount of drama and calls attention to the height of the space and the skylight above the island.

GENERAL LIGHTING

Also known as ambient lighting, general lighting is the all-purpose background light of a room. It can come from a decorative ceiling fixture, recessed lighting ("cans" that are flush mounted in the ceiling), or track systems. In any case, for general lighting you'll want either regular or "flood" bulbs, which shine with diffused light. Dimmer switches are also a good idea for these fixtures because they provide the opportunity to change the mood of the space. For example, you might want soft lighting for a casual dinner at the kitchen table but maximum brightness when you're cleaning up afterward.

above • All elements in this retro-style kitchen fit the design theme, from the square knobs on the cabinets to the color palette to the dome lights on the ceiling.

right • Absent of any light-diffusing window treatments, these windows provide plenty of natural light into this open kitchen and allow people sitting at the island to take in the beautiful view. Small ambient lights are all that's needed to supplement the natural light.

facing page top • General lighting is provided by recessed cans scattered around this kitchen. When wired to more than one switch, lights like these can be alternately turned off when this much brightness isn't needed. Better yet, use a dimmer switch to create the mood you're after.

facing page bottom • A hanging light fixture and uplights on top of the cabinets reflect plenty of light off the stainless cabinets. Supplemental light comes from the task lighting under the cabinets.

Ambient Lighting

Ambient lighting provides general, overall lighting in a room and creates a warm atmosphere. In the past, a large decorative light hung squarely in the center of the kitchen accomplished this goal. But today there are a variety of different fixtures to choose from and more creative locations to install them, such as above and below cabinetry and over tables and islands. Oftentimes, ambient lighting is a combination of two or more types of fixtures—for example, pendant-style lights and recessed downlights.

1. Recessed downlights and reproduction schoolhouse light fixtures provide ambient lighting in this kitchen. The vintage-style fixtures above the sink and island add a decorative, nostalgic element to the room. **2.** Windows at the top of the wall let in plenty of light in this basement kitchen. During the evening, however, recessed cans illuminate the space. **3.** The large ceiling fixture hangs down a bit from the ceiling, allowing the light to be diffused across the ceiling and reflect off the glass doors on the cabinets. If the fixture were closer to the ceiling it wouldn't provide as much light. **4.** Installed around the perimeter of the room, adjustable recessed downlights bounce general light off the crisp white cabinetry and into the room. In addition, they accent the decorative display above the range. Pendants over the island provide both general and task lighting. **5.** A combination of natural and artificial light is always best when it's available. Here natural light and the view from the windows and skylights take center stage. Because the eating area is open to the kitchen, the working areas are flooded with natural light as well.

TASK LIGHTING

Task lights direct their energy right onto the work surfaces of the kitchen, helping the chef see what he or she is doing without causing eye strain or shadows. You can create task lighting with hidden under-cabinet products, recessed ceiling lights, dangling pendants, or virtually any fixture that's aimed at your countertops and loaded with "spot" bulbs set at the proper distance.

above • These three pendant lights outfitted with hand-blown glass shades in a warm yellow hue add a hint of color to this otherwise black and white space. Spaced evenly above the granite island, they illuminate both the sink and the eating area.

right • A pair of hanging pendant lights with frosted shades illuminates this island. Their nickel finish harmonizes with the cup pulls on the cabinetry as well as with the prep sink in the island.

facing page top • Modern in design, these three egg-shaped fixtures provide sufficient lighting for kitchen prep work and eating. Opaque shades prevent the glaring reflection in the granite countertop that clear shades would have caused.

facing page bottom • Many range hoods are now available with built-in task lights, and some offer a choice of fluorescent or halogen, a great way to combine efficiency in a much-used work area.

Task Lighting

Task lighting illuminates work surfaces for efficiency and safety without creating shadows. It's the light you switch on when you're using sharp knives at the counter, searching for an item in the pantry, or washing dishes at the sink. Well-placed recessed downlights often provide the best task lighting, but lighting strips placed under wall cabinets and pendant fixtures spaced evenly above an island or peninsula also provide task lighting. To prevent working in shadows, use two or more adjustable fixtures to light the same surface from different directions.

1. Oblong undercabinet lights with individual switches allow light to be used where it's needed most. Puck lights or low-voltage lineal lighting (small lights running the full width of the cabinet) would have also been effective. **2.** Recessed lights wash the front of the cabinetry while casting light on the most important part of the countertop—the front half, which is the space you use the most. Avoid positioning them over aisles where they'll shine from behind you, leaving your work area in shadow. **3.** Hidden downlights under the massive hood reflect off the granite backsplash and don't detract from the beauty of the cabinetry and granite. **4.** This reproduction oil lamp casts direct light on the sink area and surrounding soapstone countertops for heavy-duty tasks. The fixture is fitted with an opaque shade to reduce nighttime reflection in the windows. **5.** Pendants are not only great over islands but also work well in front of windows, if they are outfitted with frosted or opaque shades to prevent glare. Here, the dark finish of the fixtures complements the black stone counters and the appliances.

ACCENT LIGHTING

Lighting can also be used as a design element to focus attention on a piece of artwork, an architectural feature of the kitchen, or on the fixture itself. A light placed inside an open cabinet, for example, can highlight the china displayed inside, or a pair of 1920s wall sconces might flank an antique Hoosier baking cabinet. Any type of fixture can provide accent lighting, and you don't even need lights designed solely as accents; general and task fixtures can do double-duty as accent lighting. Undercabinet lights, for example, can lend drama to a translucent glass backsplash even as they brighten your cutting boards, and sleek monorail track lighting can offer stunning visual interest that also lights up your breakfast bar peninsula.

above • Undercabinet lights are spaced at regular intervals and couple with the stainless backsplash to reflect plenty of light onto the countertop.

right • A decorative fixture reminiscent of a massive tangle of lights captures the eye in this space with vaulted ceilings.

Light Bulbs

Today's market offers a variety of light bulbs. Each kitchen fixture will come with specifications listing the type of light bulb and appropriate wattage needed. Before buying a kitchen fixture, consider the following light bulb features.

INCANDESCENT

- Casts a warm, soft glow.
- Appropriate for both ambient and task lighting.
- Lasts between 750 hours and 1,000 hours.
- Works well with dimmers.

HALOGEN

- Produces bright, clear white light.
- Brings out the depth and sparkle of granite counters.
- More energy efficient than incandescent; lasts between 2,250 hours and 3,500 hours.
- Burns hot; can be a fire hazard.

XENON

- Produces bright, clear white light.
- Brings out the depth and sparkle of granite counters.
- More energy efficient than incandescent; lasts between 2,250 hours and 3,500 hours.
- Burns a little cooler than halogen.

FLUORESCENT

- Gives off a pure white light.
- Available in a variety of colors, types, and sizes.
- The most energy efficient; can last over 10,000 hours.
- Basic, utilitarian task lighting.

Accent Lighting

Accent lighting draws and dazzles the eye. Decorative in nature, these fixtures are used to accentuate a detail such as a custom tile backsplash, a colorful or textured wall, or custom cabinetry with architectural trim such as pilasters or other embellishments. Common accent lights include adjustable track, cable, and rail systems as well as wall sconces. Small halogen recessed lights are another alternative. Installed behind glass cabinet doors, they beautifully highlight glassware, china, or pottery.

1. With their yellow glass, these period fixtures reflect the style of the kitchen but also provide a touch of diffused light. 2. Custom cabinetry, which divides this kitchen from the nearby living area, makes a bold statement with an arched soffit bridged between two half-columns. Three downlights call attention to the architecture of the piece. 3. Halogen puck lights installed in glass cabinetry can add a feeling of spaciousness to a room. They visually increase the depth of this kitchen as well as draw the eye to a set of crystal stemware and assorted decorative objects. 4. Although unusual, a lamp can function in the kitchen as well as in a family room for a touch of light as well as design interest. 5. Undercabinet lights on each side of the range accent an assortment of spice jars. Above the refrigerator, accent lighting illuminates the open shelves and highlights a display of colorful bowls.

Coloring the Walls

The color of your walls will be just as important to the overall feel of your kitchen as the color of your cabinetry, countertops, and appliances. But because the walls are relatively easy to repaint or repaper, it's a good idea to let them follow the lead of the more permanent features. If your cabinets and countertops are neutral colors (such as off-white, gray, beige, tan, or light wood and stone), you can go just about anywhere with your wall colors. After all, with so much cabinetry covering the walls (and usually a lot of windows too), even a strong color won't overpower the space. Or you can choose neutral walls as well, and let your accessories, rugs, and window treatments bring splashes of color to the space. If, on the other hand, you have selected vibrant colors for your cabinets and countertops, you'll want something more subdued for your walls in a complementary color. For example, cherry cabinetry and deep green granite countertops might call for walls of light green or yellow.

above • Who could ever imagine purple kitchen cabinets? They work in this kitchen because their vibrant color is allowed to stand on its own. Coupled with lots of glass accents and contemporary styling, this futuristic-looking kitchen is dramatic.

left • Most of us would cringe at the thought of forest green walls in any room, let alone the kitchen. But there's no arguing that here they make a dramatic statement. The color also makes the room appear much larger than it actually is.

facing page • One of the easiest ways to refresh a kitchen is by adding a few coats of paint. Here, a very simple space wrapped in robin's egg blue takes on new life.

above • A collection of dishware adds color here. Decorating with collections of things you love, from glasses to spoons to old tins, adds personality as well.

below • Spice up your kitchen with wall paint in a bold, bright color. In this space, paprika red pops the white cabinetry off the wall. Together, the red walls and the black granite counters add a sense of drama to this otherwise traditional-style room.

Simple Decor
Makes Color Pop

The simple color scheme in this kitchen in a seaside Maine home makes the room carefree, inviting, and comfortable—just what the homeowners wanted.

The contemporary, white laminate, frameless cabinetry is straightforward. Drawers under the breakfast bar provide utensil and table linen storage for the adjacent dining area. Blue laminate countertops add a punch of strong color and set the palette in motion. The blue hue appears again in the center dot of the ceramic tile floors and once again in the geometric floral patterned blue, yellow, and white tile backsplash. Simple elegance is achieved by bringing together many different bright, easy-care, and unassuming materials.

above • Taking center stage is a full-height geometric tile backsplash. A coordinating 4-in.-high tile border serves as short backsplash around the perimeter of the counter space and weds the blue in the tile to the blue laminate counters.

left • Clean and simple white laminate cabinetry combines tastefully with bright blue laminate counters and a colorful tile backsplash. The mix of simple materials creates a timeless, contemporary design.

Hand-Painted Cabinetry

There are several ways to finish wood cabinetry. You can leave it natural to show off the wood's natural grain or you can apply a coat of solid paint. But here's another choice: Have your cabinets hand-painted in contrasting colors. By using a variety of hues—pale blue, deeper blue, and light yellow—the homeowner not only adds personality to the space but also calls attention to the cabinetry's custom-crafted details.

Test your color scheme by applying the paint or wallpaper to a small area of the room. Some paint manufacturers now offer 2-oz. sample jars designed just for this purpose. If you can't obtain a wallpaper sample, purchase a single roll and tack some pieces on the walls for a few days. With wallpaper, in addition to selecting the right color, you also need to look for the right pattern or print. If the paper is too busy it will distract from the other elements of your kitchen. Keep it simple.

Also, consider durability when choosing paint or paper. For paint, eggshell or matte finishes are lovely to look at and are better at hiding wall imperfections; however, if you anticipate the need to scrub your walls periodically, consider either satin or semigloss, which are easier to keep clean. For wallpaper, look for a vinyl product. They're available in hundreds of traditional and contemporary patterns and have a waterproof coating that allows them to stand up to the humidity, spatters, and splashes of the kitchen.

above • Although the red cabinetry takes center stage in this kitchen, it doesn't overwhelm it. Natural light, reflective countertops, and interesting cutouts in the cabinets allow other colors to splash through, providing resting spaces for the eye.

right • Despite its name, wallpaper isn't just for walls. Here, a sunny yellow and white-gingham-checked print covers the walls as well as the ceiling. This type of treatment often makes a room feel cozy and intimate.

facing page • Wall color can completely change the look of any space. The green walls in this corner make the white cabinets seem brighter and more contemporary than their traditional styling would have been if the walls had been painted a neutral color. Splashes of red and yellow add interest.

Window Treatments

Some people skip the window treatments for their kitchens since privacy is usually not an issue in this room, but shades, curtains, and valances are about more than just discretion. They offer an opportunity to add additional design elements to the space. By choosing a fabric that picks up the colors used throughout the room, you can help unify the kitchen design. And consider purchasing additional yardage of your curtain fabric, if it's available, to use throughout the room. Cushions for stools, throw pillows for banquettes, and table linens can all be sewn from matching (or harmonizing) fabrics. The result will be a polished, put-together kitchen.

above • When raised, these grass blinds in an earthy tone allow diners a view of the outdoors. During especially bright days, the blinds are lowered to offer relief from the hot, glaring sun.

above right • This valance has deep balloons, allowing more of the fabric to show and cover the window. The pattern is complementary to the kitchen, though fairly subdued, allowing the accent rugs and wall decor to be colorful focal points.

below right • Honeycomb shades can be coupled with a valance, or other treatment, or left alone as was done here. The white color blends with the cabinetry and helps contribute to the clean look of this kitchen.

facing page • The blue print fabric of this window treatment enhances the granite countertops and creates a striking contrast to the rich cherry cabinetry.

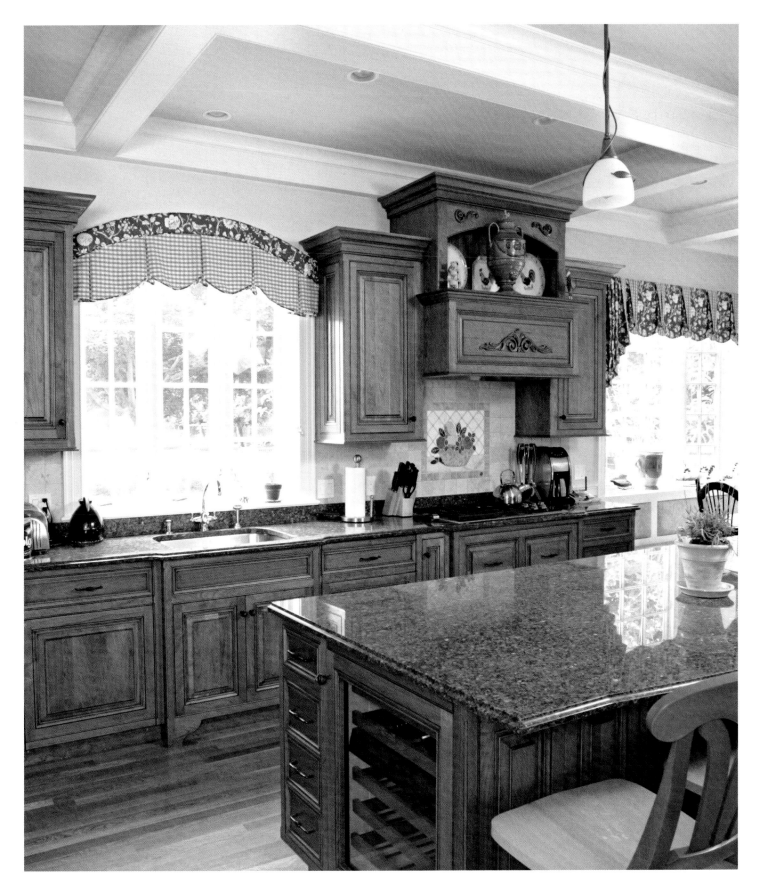

Seating

Every kitchen needs seating. It might come in the form of a kitchenette set, a built-in restaurant-style booth, or the most popular option by far: a breakfast bar where you can pull up stools to a counter. Bar stools are space efficient because they can be stowed under the counter when not in use, and they provide a convenient perch for eating a snack, sitting down to cook, or for family members and guests to hang out and watch you work. Whether you want stools that swivel, have backs and arms, or upholstered seats, you can find numerous choices at furniture stores, kitchen specialty shops, and even on the Web. Just make sure to get stools with seats that are about 12 in. lower than your countertops. Most often, bar counters are set at 42 in. (well above the standard countertop height), so the seats should be about 30 in. off the floor. And at that height, foot rests will make the stools a lot more comfortable. Counter-height bars are set at 36 in. off the floor and require stools with seats that are 24 in. high.

above • Low bar stools that fit under the countertop work perfectly here. Not only do they add seating while dinner is being prepared but they allow the chef to see into the adjacent space without a chair back interfering with the view.

left • Built-in seating provides a casual feeling to this eating area. The round table prevents the area from feeling too boxy and allows multiple chairs to be pulled up as needed.

facing page • Upholstered seating is designed to invite the diner to relax. Because the table has no apron, it can be moved closer to the bench as needed without hitting anyone's knees.

Using Color to Refresh an Old Kitchen

The homeowners of this 1930s English Tudor in the California countryside fell in love with the house but not with the kitchen. Although it had been remodeled in the 1990s, it didn't reflect their personality and sense of style. The white painted cabinetry was fine quality, the countertops were white ceramic tile, and the white oak strip flooring was in good condition. In short, the kitchen was just too nice to consider ripping it out and starting over. Their plan was simple: new paint, new countertops, and a few new appliances.

The island was painted apple green with burnt umber glazing, and the wall cabinets were done in a chambray blue. The base cabinets were painted in a deeper shade of blue. Adding glass doors to the wall cabinets gave the space an open and airy feel and allowed the display of cherished pieces.

The original white tile countertop was retained on either side of the range for its ability to catch bubbling hot dishes from the oven. Other areas were treated with new countertops: The island was topped with honed limestone, and the remaining countertops were done in maple butcher block. The original range was kept, but the stainless-steel refrigerator and dishwasher are new.

Using yellow, green, and blue paint to match the cabinetry, the designer fashioned a plaid pattern on the floor, which was then covered with several coats of protective urethane. The result is a successful marriage of complementary materials that provide a cheery, fresh face for this kitchen.

To reflect their personal style without spending a lot of money, the owners of this kitchen repainted the existing cabinetry in pastel green and blue. Stainless-steel appliances and glass-fronted white cabinets contribute to the fresh appeal of the space.

top · This kitchen is well detailed in the retro style, from the appliances to the glass block and tiles all around the room. The wrought-iron café table and chairs work well in the small eating alcove.

above · Long-legged and spindly, these barstools fit in well with the open, airy feeling of this bright space. The two-tone color of the stools harmonizes with the white cabinetry and the tile floor, too.

Bar Stools

Bar stools come in myriad styles and shapes. They can be hidden underneath a counter extension or overhang until needed or cause a design stir all on their own. The primary function of this furniture is seating, though, so keep this in mind when shopping. Also think about how the stools will be used in the kitchen: as primary or secondary seating, for eating or chatting, for homework or bill paying. The end use also has ramifications on how high the stools should be, whether you want them with a back, and how many you might need.

1. The warm wood tones of these petite stools complement with the pale yellow walls and coordinate with the wood floor. When space is limited, this type of stool can allow maximum seating since it tucks neatly under the counter space. 2. Contemporary-style barstools blend beautifully with the maple cabinetry and black granite in this kitchen. The half-moon shape of the stool's back is a pleasant addition to a room of mostly angular forms. 3. In a room made up of smooth surfaces, the woven seats of these simple, backless barstools provide a much-needed dose of texture. Their pale frames complement the cabinetry in a natural finish and the island topped with maple butcher block.

4

5

6

4. The shapely form of this bentwood barstool stands out sharply against a backdrop of simple fixtures and materials. **5.** The woven seats and metal legs make these bar stools fun and flexible, conforming to people of varying sizes. They tuck under the counter when not in use. **6.** The spindles on the backs of these bar stools mimic the other lines in the room, including the window panes, wainscot on the walls, ceiling, and louvered doors on the cabinets.

Accessorizing

Adding your personality to your kitchen is something you'll probably do throughout the process of choosing materials and components. But adding accessories—such as a throw rug, flea-market spice rack, wall art, or a treasured collection—can also make the space uniquely yours. The good news about these embellishments is that they don't have to be permanent, so you can swap them with the seasons, as your tastes change, or when your kids bring home new artwork.

above • Practical as well as visually interesting, the magnetic strips attached to the refrigerator cabinets hold small metal spice boxes.

left • This appealing decorative display of glass jars adds a splash of color against the white walls. The varying shapes and sizes add further interest.

right • The whimsical rug in this cheery space coordinates with the blue and yellow colors of the nearby chairs. An accent piece such as this provides a simple way to alter the color scheme of a room without breaking the bank.

facing page top • The style of this country kitchen is emphasized with a blue-patterned tile backsplash and yellow shelves. A collection of dog figurines fits right in with the eclectic feeling of this kitchen.

facing page bottom • Adding a pot rack is a way to accessorize with practicality in mind. This wrought-iron version harmonizes with the dark finish on the base of the center island and the black soapstone counters on either side of the sink.

Pot Racks

A pot rack should first be a decorative element and second an organizational tool for your cookware. The best location for a rack is above an island or peninsula where the likelihood of bumping your head is slim. Before you install a pot rack, though, consider how it will affect your lighting needs. Fixtures such as pendant lights, for example, will compete for ceiling space. To avoid the two getting in each other's way, some manufacturers incorporate downlights into their racks. Another option: Have your electrical contractor install recessed lighting in the ceiling. Just make sure the beam of light won't be interrupted by dangling pots and pans.

1. Pot racks positioned over islands or peninsulas offer bonus storage for some of the most-used items in the kitchen. This black wrought-iron example allows light to shine through. **2.** Pot racks don't have to hold every pot you'll ever need. This small one is finely detailed and gets a good deal of attention since it's positioned directly under a recessed light. **3.** Rather than install costly wall cabinets, the budget-conscious owner of this remodeled space installed a handsome wall-hung pot rack.

4. Suspended with chains over the center island, this custom pot rack made in the same warm cherry as the kitchen cabinetry puts pots and pans well within reach of the cook. **5.** Sliding hooks on this rack allow pots of various sizes to be accommodated. When installed on a wall like this one tall people don't have to worry about bumping into it. **6.** Gleaming copper pots and pans are at the ready in this chef's kitchen. The clean lines of the pot rack and holders mimic the rest of the kitchen.

Organizations

**AMERICAN INSTITUTE
OF ARCHITECTS (AIA)**
1735 New York Ave. NW
Washington, DC 20006-5292
202-626-7300; 800-AIA-3837
www.aia.org

**NATIONAL KITCHEN AND
BATH ASSOCIATION (NKBA)**
687 Willow Grove St.
Hackettstown, NJ 07840
800-843-6522
www.nkba.org

Manufacturers

Appliances

AMANA
Maytag Customer Service
403 West Fourth St. N
Newton, IA 50208
800-843-0304
www.amana.com

BEST HOODS
Broan-Nutone, LLC
926 West State St.
Hartford, WI 53027
800-558-1711
www.bestbybroan.com

DACOR
1440 Bridge Gate Dr.
Diamond Bar, CA 91765
800-793-0093
ww2.dacor.com

FISHER & PAYKEL APPLIANCES
U.S. and Canada Headquarters
5900 Skylab Rd.
Huntington Beach, CA 92647
1-888-936-7872
www.usa.fisherpaykel.com

GENERAL ELECTRIC
Appliance Headquarters
AP 6 Room 129
Louisville, KY 40225
800-626-2005
www.geappliances.com

KITCHEN-AID
P.O. Box 218
St. Joseph, MI 49085
800-422-1230
www.kitchenaid.com

LG ELECTRONICS
U.S.A. Corporate Headquarters
1000 Sylvan Ave.
Englewood Cliffs, NJ 07632
800-243-0000
us.lge.com

MAYTAG APPLIANCES
240 Edwards St.
Cleveland, TN 37311
800-688-9900
www.maytag.com

MIELE
9 Independence Way
Princeton, NJ 08540
800-843-7231
www.miele.com

SHARP ELECTRONICS CORP.
Sharp Plaza
Mahwah, NJ 07430
201-529-8200; 800-BE-SHARP
www.sharpusa.com

SUB-ZERO FREEZER CO., INC.
P.O. Box 44988
Madison, WI 53744-4988
800-222-7820
www.subzero.com

THERMADOR
5551 McFadden Ave.
Huntington Beach, CA 92649
800-735-5547
www.thermador.com

VENT-A-HOOD®
P.O. Box 830426
Richardson, TX 75083-0426
800-331-2492
www.ventahood.com

VIKING RANGE CORP.
111 Front St.
Greenwood, MS 38930
662-455-1200; 800-VIKING1
www.vikingrange.com

WOLF APPLIANCE COMPANY, LLC
P.O. Box 44988
Madison, WI 53744-4988
800-222-7820
www.subzero.com

ZEPHYR VENTILATION
395 Mendell St.
San Francisco, CA 94124
888-880-VENT
www.zephyronline.com

Cabinetry

ARISTOKRAFT CABINETRY
One Masterbrand Cabinets Dr.
P.O. Box 420
Jasper, IN 47547-0420
812-482-6566
www.aristokraft.com

KOUNTRY KRAFT, INC.
P.O. Box 570
291 South Sheridan Rd.
Newmanstown, PA 17073
610-589-4575
www.kountrykraft.com

KRAFTMAID CABINETRY
P.O. Box 1055
15535 South State Ave.
Middlefield, OH 44062
440-632-5333
www.kraftmaid.com

THOMASVILLE CABINETRY
800-756-6497
www.thomasville.com

**WOOD-MODE
FINE CUSTOM CABINETRY**
One Second St.
Kreamer, PA 17833
877-635-7500
www.wood-mode.com

Sinks and Faucets

AMERICAN STANDARD
P.O. Box 6820
1 Centennial Plaza
Piscataway, NJ 08855-6820
800-442-1902
www.americanstandard-us.com

BLANCO AMERICA, INC.
110 Mount Holly By-Pass
Lumberton, NJ 08048
www.blancoamerica.com

CHICAGO FAUCETS
2100 South Clearwater Dr.
Des Plaines, IL 60018-5999
847-803-5000
www.chicagofaucets.com

DELTA FAUCET CO.
55 East 111th St.
P.O. Box 40980
Indianapolis, IN 46280
800-345-DELTA
www.deltafaucet.com

ELKAY
2222 Camden Ct.
Oak Brook, IL 60523
630-574-8484
www.elkay.com

**FRANKE CONSUMER
PRODUCTS, INC.**
Kitchen Systems Division
3050 Campus Dr., Suite 500
Hatfield, PA 19440
800-626-5771
www.frankeksd.com

HANSGROHE, INC.
1490 Bluegrass Lakes Pkwy.
Alpharetta, GA 30004
800-488-8119
www.hansgrohe-usa.com

JUST SINKS
Just Manufacturing
9233 King St.
Franklin Park, IL 60131
847-678-5150
www.justsinks.com

KOHLER
444 Highland Dr.
Kohler, WI 53044
800-4-KOHLER
www.kohler.com

KWC FAUCETS
1770 Corporate Dr. #580
Norcross, GA 30093
678-334-2121
www.kwcfaucets.com

MOEN INC.
25300 Al Moen Dr.
North Olmsted, OH 44070
800-BUY-MOEN
www.moen.com

Countertops

CAESARSTONE
11830 Sheldon St.
Sun Valley, CA 91352
818-394-6000; 877-9QUARTZ
www.ceasartoneus.com

DUPONT SURFACES
Chestnut Run Plaza, Bldg. 721
P.O. Box 80721
Wilmington, DE 19880
800-426-7426
www.corian.com

**FERAZZOLI IMPORTS
OF NEW ENGLAND, INC.**
234 Middle St.
Middletown, CT 06457
860-346-1923; 800-235-3463
www.ferazzoli-imports.com

JOHN BOOS & CO.
P.O. Box 609
315 South First St.
Effingham, IL 62401
217-347-7701
www.johnboos.com

JUST STAINLESS STEEL
Just Manufacturing
9233 King St.
Franklin Park, IL 60131
847-678-5150
www.justmfg.com

VERMONT SOAPSTONE
P.O. Box 268
Perkinsville, VT 05151
802-263-5404
www.vermontsoapstone.com

Flooring

ARMSTRONG
Armstrong World Industries
P.O. Box 3001
Lancaster, PA 17604
717-397-0611
www.armstrong.com

DUPONT LAMINATE
Chestnut Run Plaza, Bldg. 721
P.O. Box 80721
Wilmington, DE 19880
877-438-6824
www.flooring.dupont.com

WICANDERS CORK FLOORING
Amorim Flooring North America
7513 Connelley Dr., Suite M
Hanover, MD 21076
410-553-6062
www.wicanders.com

Lighting

HALO
Cooper Lighting
1121 Highway 74 S
Peachtree City, GA 30269
www.cooperlighting.com

JUNO
www.junolighting.com

LIGHTOLIER
631 Airport Rd.
Fall River, MA 02720
508-679-8131
www.lightolier.com

QUOIZEL
590 Old Willets Path
Hauppauge, NY 11788
631-273-2700
www.quoizel.com

SEAGULL
310 West Washington St.
Riverside, NJ 08075
800-347-5483
www.seagulllighting.com

Internet Resources

**AMERICAN LIGHTING
ASSOCIATION**
*This Web site offers a search engine
for finding local members of the
association who are knowledgeable
about lighting design. The site also
provides articles with tips on lighting
kitchens as well as other rooms in
the home.*
www.americanlightingassoc.com

BUILD.COM
*This Web site offers one-stop shopping
for many hard-to-find items, such
as pot racks, soap dispensers, and
cutting boards. Plumbing and lighting
supplies are also available here.*
www.build.com

ENERGYSTAR
*This Web site is offered by the U.S.
federal government and provides
information about many energy-
related issues, including articles on
obtaining tax credits for purchasing
energy-efficient products. The site also
includes information about the Energy
Star rating.*
www.energystar.gov

HGTV
*This is the Web site of the Home
and Garden Television Network.
Besides offering a television schedule
indicating when shows concentrating
on kitchen design will be aired, the
site provides information about the
products featured on those shows.
HGTV has posted numerous articles
on planning kitchens, including an
online design tool for creating a basic
kitchen floor plan.*
www.hgtv.com

HOME APPLIANCE MAGAZINE
*Home Appliance magazine offers
product reviews for a variety of
appliances, from ranges to portable
air-conditioners.*
www.appliance.com

HOME PORTFOLIO
*This Web site offers a powerful search
engine for creating a portfolio of
design ideas. The system speeds up the
design, research, and decision-making
processes and provides information
about available options. Kitchens,
baths, and other rooms of the home
are featured.*
www.homeportfolio.com

IFLOOR.COM
*This Web site is an online store
featuring all types of flooring, from
traditional materials like carpeting
and hardwood to the latest
developments like bamboo and cork.*
www.ifloor.com

KITCHENS.COM
*Chockfull of tips and information
about kitchen styles and trends, this
Web site includes a photo gallery for
ideas. A dealer locater, by ZIP code is
also available.*
www.kitchens.com

OIKOS
*This is an online newsletter that
provides information about green
living and building. The site offers
articles on green products and sells
books through an online bookstore.*
oikos.com

PERIOD HOMES MAGAZINE
Period Homes *magazine provides
resources for professionals working
on traditionally styled homes. There
is useful information for restoration
and renovation projects as well as
historically inspired new construction.*
www.period-homes.com

SUPER KITCHENS
*This Web site offers practical advice
and remodeling ideas for kitchen
planning and storage solutions.
Links to the Web sites of kitchen
product manufacturers are provided.*
www.superkitchens.com

CREDITS

p. 4: © Mark Lohman

p. 6: Top: © Mark Lohman; design: Janet Lohman Interior Design; bottom: © Alise O'Brien, design: CLB Design

p. 7: © Mark Lohman

p. 8: Left: Charles Miller, © The Taunton Press, Inc.; right: © Rob Karosis

p. 9: © Ken Gutmaker

p. 10: Top and bottom: © Eric Roth; design: Tom Catalano, Catalano Architects

p. 11: © Eric Roth; design: Tom Catalano, Catalano Architects

p. 12: Left: © Mark Lohman; design: Janet Lohman Interior Design, Los Angeles, CA; right: © Mark Lohman; design: Lynn Pries Design, Newport Beach, CA

p. 14: Top and bottom: © Grey Crawford

p. 15: Courtesy Mosaik Design

p. 16: © Mark Lohman

p. 17: © Ken Gutmaker

p. 18-19: Courtesy Kitchens by Deane/www.kitchensbydeane.com; design: Alice Hayes

p. 20: Top: © Mark Samu/www.samustudios.com; design: Donald Billinkoff AIA; bottom: © Rob Karosis

p. 21: Top: Charles Miller © The Taunton Press, Inc.; bottom: Mike Moore © The Taunton Press, Inc.

p. 22: © Mark Samu/www.samustudios.com; design: Correia Design

p. 23: © Rob Karosis; design: Rick Harlan Schneider, AIA

p. 24: © Eric Roth

p. 26: Top: © Grey Crawford; bottom: © Mark Lohman; design: Douglas Burdge Architects

p. 27 Charles Bickford, © The Taunton Press, Inc.

p. 28: © Alise O'Brien; design: European Bath, Kitchen, Tile and Stone

p. 29: Top: courtesy Mosaik Design; bottom: © Scot Zimmerman; design: Bud Bracken Builders

p. 30: © Anne Gummerson; design: Laura Thomas, Melville-Thomas Architects

p. 31: © Anne Gummerson; design: Laura Thomas, Melville-Thomas Architects

p. 32: Top: © Mark Lohman; bottom: © James Shive; design: Castle Contractors

p. 33: © Eric Roth; design: David Pill

p. 36: Top: © Eric Roth; bottom: © Brian Vanden Brink; design: Stephen Blatt Architects

p. 37: © Linda Svendsen

p. 38: © J.R. Emmanuelli; design: Beth Veillette, Hanford Cabinet & Woodworking, Inc.

p. 39: © J.R. Emmanuelli; design: Beth Veillette, Hanford Cabinet & Woodworking, Inc.

p. 40: © Rob Karosis

p 41: Top: © Brian Vanden Brink; bottom: © Grey Crawford

p. 42: Right: © David Duncan Livingston; left: © Olson Photographic/www.olsonphotographic.com; design: EHL Kitchens

p. 43: © Mark Lohman; design: Cheryl Hamilton-Gray, Oceanside, CA

p. 44: Top: © Mark Lohman; design: Lynn Pries Design; bottom: left © Sara Hanford, design: Steve Hanford, Hanford Cabinet & Woodworking, Inc.; bottom right Roe Osborn © The Taunton Press, Inc.

p. 45: © Brian Vanden Brink; design: John Morris, Architect

p. 46: © Chipper Hatter; design: Richard Ourso Design

p. 47: © Chipper Hatter; design: Richard Ourso Design

p. 48: Top: © Anne Gummerson; design: Beth Fannin, Myamoto Kitchen Post and Beam Construction; bottom: Margot Hartford, www.margothartford.com; design: Fox Design Group, Architects, interior design by Navarra Design

p. 49: Charles Miller © The Taunton Press, Inc.

p. 50: © Anne Gummerson; design: Jeff and Laura Penza, Penza Associates, Architects

p. 51: Top: © Brian Vanden Brink; bottom left: © James Shive; design: Aker's Custom Homes; bottom right: © Mark Samu/www.samustudios.com; design: Jean Stoffer Design

p. 52: Top: © Randy O'Rourke; bottom: © Eric Roth; design: Gracyn Whitman Design

p. 53: Olson Photographic/www.olsonphotographic.com; design: Northeast Cabinet Design

p. 54: © Brian Vanden Brink; design: Quinn Evans, Architects

p. 56: Top: courtesy Kitchens by Deane/www.kitchensbydeane.com; bottom: left © Eric Roth

p. 57: © Brian Vanden Brink

p. 58: © Brian Vanden Brink; design: Drysdale Associate Interior Design

p. 59: Top left: Margot Hartford, www.margothartford.com; design: Fox Design Group, Architects, interior design by Marilyn Davies Design; top right courtesy The Kennebec Company; bottom: © Ken Gutmaker

p. 60: Left: © Grey Crawford; right: Courtesy Woodmode Cabinetry

p. 61: Courtesy Kountry Kraft Kitchens

p. 62: Top: © Mark Lohman; center courtesy JFA Architecture, p.c.; bottom: courtesy Thomasville Cabinetry

p. 63: © Scot Zimmerman

p. 64: © Brian Vanden Brink; design: Thom Rouselle, Architect

p. 65: Top and center: © Mark Samu/www.samustudios.com; design: Jean Stoffer Design; bottom: © Linda Svendsen

p. 66-67: © Olson Photographic/www.olsonphotographic.com; design: Vic Anatra

p. 68: Top courtesy Kountry Kraft, Newmanstown, PA; bottom left: © Eric Roth; design: Mark Hammer, Hammer Architects

p. 70: Courtesy Kountry Kraft; design: Kitchen Classics by Custom Crafters

p. 71: Top right: © Eric Roth; design: King Kitchen Feinmann, Inc., Arlington, MA; bottom right: © Alise O'Brien; design: Glen Alspaugh Kitchens; left: Chris Green © The Taunton Press, Inc.

p. 72: Top: © Brian Vanden Brink; design: Centerbrook Architects; bottom left: courtesy Drury Design; bottom right: © Scot Zimmerman; design: Split Rock Design

p. 73: © Scot Zimmerman; design: Kristina Weaver/Lisman Richardson

p. 74: © Mark Lohman

p. 75: Top: © Ken Gutmaker; bottom: © Mark Lohman, design: Roxanne Packham Design

p. 76: Left: © Mark Lohman, design: Janet Lohman Interior Design, Los Angeles, CA; top right: © Mark Lohman; design: Cheryl Hamilton-Gray; bottom right: © Mark Lohman

p. 77: Top right: © Mark Samu/www.samustudios.com; design: Jean Stoffer Design; bottom right: © Eric Roth; left © Mark Lohman; design: Janet Lohman Interior Design

p. 78: Top: © Sarah B. Hanford; design: Beth Veillette, Hanford Cabinets & Woodworking, Inc.; bottom left: courtesy Kountry Kraft; bottom right © Ken Gutmaker

p. 79: © Eric Roth; design: Astrid Vigeland

p. 80-81: © Brian Vanden Brink

p. 82: Top: © Mark Samu/www.samustudios.com; design: Jean Stoffer Design; bottom left: © Ken Gutmaker; bottom right: © Eric Roth, design: David Tonnesen

p. 83: © James Shive; design: Sawhorse Designs

p. 84: Top left: Margot Hartford, www.margothartford.com; design: Fox Design Group, Architects, top right: courtesy Kountry Kraft; bottom left: © Eric Roth; bottom right: © Eric Roth

p. 85: Left: © Mark Samu/www.samustudios.com; top right: courtesy Kountry Kraft; bottom right: courtesy Kountry Kraft

p. 86: Courtesy Jennifer Gilmer

p. 88: Left: © Adrianne DePolo; right: © Olson Photographic/www.olsonphotographic.com

p. 89: Top right: © James Shive; design: Sawhorse Designs; bottom right: © Sarah B. Hanford; design: Beth Veillette, Hanford Cabinets & Woodworking, Inc.

p. 90: Top: © Brian Vanden Brink; design: Design Group Three Architects; bottom: © Scot Zimmerman; design: Kristina Weaver/Lisman Richardson; right: © Tim Street-Porter

p. 91: © Mark Samu/www.samustudios.com

p. 92: Top left: © Matthew Millman; bottom left: © Ken Gutmaker; bottom right: © Brian Vanden Brink; design: Jack Silverio, Architect

p. 93: Top right: © David Duncan Livingston; center right: © Alise O'Brien; bottom right: © Linda Svendsen; design: Diamond Bullnosing/Granite; bottom left: © Brian Vanden Brink; design: Nancy Barba, Architects

p. 94: Top: © James Shive; design: Sawhorse Designs; bottom: © Mark Samu/www.samustudios.com

p. 95: © Randy O'Rourke

p. 96-97: © Sarah B. Hanford; design: Beth Veillette, Hanford Cabinets & Woodworking, Inc.

p. 98: Top: © Olson Photographic/www.olsonphotographic.com; design: The Kitchen Company; bottom left: © Eric Roth; design: Tom Catalano, Catalano Architects; bottom right: © Brian Vanden Brink; design: Susan Thorn, Interior Design

p. 99: © Olson Photographic/www.olsonphotographic.com; design: Amazing Spaces, Briarcliff Manor, NY

p. 100: Left: © Eric Roth; right: © Paul Bardagjy

p. 101: Top: © Fu-Tung Cheng; bottom: © Matthew Millman

p. 102: Top: © Grey Crawford; bottom left: © Grey Crawford; bottom right: © Ken Gutmaker

p. 103: © Mark Lohman

p. 104-105: Courtesy Kitchens by Deane/www.kitchensbydeane.com; design: Carrie Deane Corcoran

p. 106: Left: © Chipper Hatter; right: © Scot Zimmerman; design: Split Rock Design

p. 107: © Grey Crawford

p. 108: Top right: © Mark Lohman; bottom right: © Eric Roth, design: Molly Moran Architect; left: © Ken Gutmaker

p. 109: © Brian Vanden Brink; design: Dominic Mercadante, Architect

p. 110: Left: © Ken Gutmaker; right: © Rob Karosis

p. 111: Top: © Roger Turk/Northlight Photography; bottom: © Rob Karosis

p. 112: © Mark Lohman; design: Susan Philipp Design

p. 114: Top: © Brian Vanden Brink; bottom: © Rob Karosis; Jonathan Barnes, AIA NCARB

p. 115: © Mark Samu/www.samustudios.com; design: Jean Stoffer Design

p. 116: left: © Carolyn Bates/www.carolynbates.com; design: Robyn Fairclough; right: © Olson Photographic/www.olsonphotographic.com; design: A Matter of Style

p. 117: Top: © Alise O'Brien; bottom: © Mark Lohman

p. 118-: © Rob Karosis; design: Mark Stein, Stein Troost Architects

p. 119: Top left: © Brian Vanden Brink; design: Morningstar Marble & Granite; top right: © Ken Gutmaker; © Mark Lohman; design: Janet Lohman Interior Design

p. 120: © Mark Lohman; design: Susan Cohen Design

p. 121: Top: © Mark Lohman; design: Lynn Pies; bottom: © Matthew Millman

p. 122-123: © Sarah B. Hanford; design: Beth Veillette, Hanford Cabinet & Woodworking, Inc.

p. 124: Top: © Rob Karosis; bottom: © Anne Gummerson, design: Joe Gilday, Fineberg Gilday Renovations

p. 125: Courtesy Jennifer Gilmer Kitchens

p. 126: Courtesy Kitchens by Deane/www.kitchensbydeane.com; design: Carrie Deane Corcoran

p. 127: © Mick Hales

p. 128: © Carolyn Bates/www.carolynbates.com

p. 129: Top left: © Brian Vanden Brink; design: Elliott Elliott Norelius Architects; top right: © Anne Gummerson; bottom: © Ken Gutmaker

p. 130: © James Shive; design: Sawhorse Designs

p. 131: Top: © Mark Lohman; bottom: © Linda Svendsen; design: Premier Kitchens

p. 132: © Mark Samu/www.samustudios.com; design: Jean Stoffer Design

p. 133: Top: © Mark Lohman; bottom: © Matthew Millman; right courtesy Jennifer Gilmer Kitchens

p. 134-135: © Eric Roth; design: Kathleen Sullivan Elliot Interior Design

p. 136: Top: courtesy Jennifer Gilmer Kitchens; bottom right: © Eric Roth; bottom left: © Mark Lohman

p. 137: Courtesy Jennifer Gilmer Kitchens

p. 138: © Brian Vanden Brink; design: Morningstar Marble & Granite

p. 139: Top: Kent Peterson; center © Ken Gutmaker; bottom: © Mark Lohman

p. 140: Top right: Courtesy Kitchens by Deane/www.kitchensbydeane.com; design: Carrie Deane Corcoran; bottom left: © Sarah B. Hanford; design: Steve Hanford, Hanford Cabinet & Woodworking, Inc.; bottom right: Chris Green © The Taunton Press, Inc.

p. 141: © James Shive, design: Sawhorse Designs

p. 142: Courtesy Kountry Kraft

p. 144-145: © Mark Lohman

p. 145: Top right: Charles Miller © The Taunton Press, Inc.; bottom right: © Eric Roth; design: Benjamin Nutter Architects

p. 146: © Sarah Hanford; design: Beth Veillette, Hanford Cabinet & Woodworking, Inc.

p. 147: Top: © Grey Crawford; bottom: © Brian Vanden Brink; design: Elliott Elliott Norelius Architects

p. 148: Courtesy Kitchens by Design

p. 149: Top: © Linda Svendsen; bottom left: © Mark Lohman; bottom right: © Matthew Millman

p. 150: Top right: © Olson Photographic/www.olsonphotographic.com; design: Betsy House Kitchen and Bath Design; bottom right: © Eric Roth; bottom left: © Mark Lohman

p. 151: © Mark Lohman; design: Cheryl Hamilton-Gray

p. 152-153: © Brian Vanden Brink

p. 154: Top: © The Taunton Press, Inc.; bottom: © David Duncan Livingston

p. 155: Left: © Randy O'Rourke; right: © Ken Gutmaker

p. 156: Left: © Olson Photographic/www.olsonphotographic.com; design: Classic Kitchens; right: © Randy O'Rourke

p. 157: Top: courtesy Armstrong Floors; bottom left: © Brian Vanden Brink; design: Dominic Mercadante, Architect; bottom right: © Brian Vanden Brink; design: Chris Glass, Architect

p. 158: © Matthew Millman

p. 159: © Matthew Millman

p. 160: Left: © Brian Vanden Brink; design: Harbor Farm Designs; right: © Mark Lohman; design: Susan Philipp Design

p. 161: Top: © Olson Photographic/www.olsonphotographic.com; design: Complete Construction; bottom: © Eric Roth

p. 162: © Chipper Hatter; design: Remson Haley Herpin Architects

p. 164: Top: courtesy Hamilton-Gray Design; bottom right: © Ken Gutmaker; Bottom left: courtesy Jennifer Gilmer Kitchens

p. 165: © Eric Roth

p. 166: Top: © Anne Gummerson; bottom: courtesy Jennifer Gilmer Kitchens

p. 167: © Mark Lohman

p. 168: © Mark Samu/www.samustudios.com

p. 168-169: Courtesy Jennifer Gilmer Kitchens

p. 170: Top: © Mark Lohman; design: Debra Jones Design; bottom: © Ken Gutmaker

p. 171: © Brian Vanden Brink, Todd Caverly Photographer; design: Rockport Post & Beam

p. 172: © Olson Photographic/www.olsonphotographic.com; design: Northeast Cabinet Design

p. 173: Top: © Olson Photographic/www.olsonphotographic.com; design: Betsy House Kitchen and Bath Design; bottom: © Sarah B. Hanford; design: Steve Hanford, Hanford Cabinet & woodworking, Inc.

p. 174: © Scot Zimmerman, design: Kelly & Shari Warnick

p. 175: © Scot Zimmerman, design: Kelly & Shari Warnick

p. 176: Top left and right: © Sarah B. Hanford; design: Beth Veillette, Hanford Cabinet & Woodworking, Inc.; bottom left and right: © Olson Photographic/www.olsonphotographic.com, design: New Canaan Kitchens

p. 177: © Brian Vanden Brink; design: John Morris, Architect

p. 178: © Alise O'Brien; design: Bentel & Bentel

p. 178-179: © Rob Karosis; design: Ralph Cunningham, AIA, Cunningham + Quill Architects, Washington, DC

p. 180: © Olson Photographic/www.olsonphotographic.com; design: Classic Kitchens

p. 180-181: Tom O'Brien, © The Taunton Press, Inc.

p. 181: © Olson Photographic/www.olsonphotographic.com; design: Classic Kitchens

p. 182: Top: courtesy Jennifer Gilmer Kitchens; bottom: © Brian Vanden Brink, design: John Martin Architect

p. 183: Left: courtesy Jennifer Gilmer Kitchens; top and bottom right: © Brian Vanden Brink

p. 184-185: © Linda Svendsen, design: Douglas Design

p. 186: Top: © Randy O'Rourke; bottom: courtesy Kitchens by Deane/www.kitchensbydeane.com, design: Carrie Deane Corcoran

p. 187: © Linda Svendsen

p. 188: Top: © Eric Roth; bottom right: © Anne Gummerson; bottom left: Paul Bardagjy

p. 189: Right: © David Duncan Livingston; left: © Scot Zimmerman

p. 190: Left: © Sarah B. Hanford; design: Beth Veillette, Hanford Cabinet & Woodworking, Inc.; right: © Ken Gutmaker

p. 191: © Ken Gutmaker

p. 192: © Anne Gummerson

p. 194: Top: © Scott Zimmerman; bottom: © Olson Photographic/www.olsonphotographic.com

p. 195: © Brian Vanden Brink; design: Siemasko & Verbridge Architects

p. 196: © Mark Lohman

p. 197: Top right: © Eric Roth; design: Stirling Brown Architects; bottom right: © Olson Photographic/www.olsonphotographic.com; left © Brian Vanden Brink

p. 198: © Mark Lohman

p. 198-199: © Brian Vanden Brink; design: John Morris Architect

p. 199: Top: Roe Osborn © The Taunton Press, Inc.; bottom right: © Eric Roth; design: Cann & Co.,

p. 200: Left: © Linda Svendsen; right: Charles Miller © The Taunton Press, Inc.

p. 201: Top left: © Scot Zimmerman; design: Jan Ledgard; top right: © Olson Photographic/www.olsonphotographic.com; design: EHL Kitchens; bottom: © Rob Karosis

p. 202: © Linda Svendsen

p. 202-203: © Brian Vanden Brink; design: Sally Weston, Architect

p. 203: Top: © Ken Gutmaker; bottom: © Mark Samu/www.samustudios.com

p. 204: Top: © Mark Lohman; design: Janet Lohman Interior Design; bottom left: © Brian Vanden Brink, design: Rob Whitten, Architect; bottom right: © Mark Lohman, design: Cheryl Hamilton-Gray

p. 205: Right: © Olson Photographic/www.olsonphotographic.com; left: © Eric Roth; right

p. 206: © Carolyn Bates/www.carolynbates.com; design: Peter Morris

p. 206-207: © Mark Lohman; design: Roxanne Packham Design

p. 208: Top: courtesy Mosaik Design; bottom left: © Eric Roth; bottom right: © Anne Gummerson

p. 209: Top: ©Chipper Hatter; bottom: © Rob Karosis; design: Pi Smith, AIA, Smith and Vansant Architects

p. 210: Top: © Carolyn Bates/www.carolynbates.com; bottom: © Brian Vanden Brink; design Pete Bethanis, Architect

p. 211: © Scot Zimmerman; design: Vickee Byrum/Yellow Door Design

p. 212: Top: © Mark Lohman; bottom: © Chipper Hatter, design: Remson Haley Herpin Architects

p. 213: © Brian Vanden Brink, design: Scholz and Barclay Architects

p. 214: Margot Hartford, www.margothartford.com; design: Fox Design Group, Architects, interior design by Marilyn Davies Design

p. 215: Top: © Chipper Hatter; bottom right: © Eric Roth; design: Gayle Jenney Interiors; bottom left: © Anne Gummerson

p. 216: Top: © Brian Vanden Brink; design: Drysdale Associate Interior Design; bottom left: © Mark Lohman; bottom right: courtesy Mosaik Design

p. 217: © Sarah B. Hanford; design: Steve Hanford, Hanford Cabinet & Woodworking, Inc.

p. 218: Courtesy Fox Design Group, Architects

p. 118-119: © Brian Vanden Brink; design: John Cole Architect

p. 119: © Brian Vanden Brink; design: Dominic Mercadante, Architect

p. 220-221: © Mark Lohman; design: Janet Lohman Interior Design, Los Angeles, CA

p. 221: Top: © Mark Lohman; bottom: © Olson Photographic/www.olsonphotographic.com; design: Peter Cadoux Architects

p. 222: Top: © Mark Samu/www.samustudios.com; design: Jean Stoffer Design; bottom left: © Anne Gummerson; bottom right: © Brian Vanden Brink; design: Scott Simons Architect

p. 223: Top left: © Eric Roth; design: Tacey Luongo Architect; Top right: © Mark Lohman, design: Roxanne Packham Design; bottom: © Brian Vanden Brink; design: Group 3 Architects

p. 224: Top: © Grey Crawford; bottom: © David Duncan Livingston

p. 225: Top right: © Eric Roth; design: Elizabeth Speert, Inc.; bottom right: © James Shive; design: Castle Contractors; left: © Alise O'Brien, design: Directions in Design,

p. 226: Top: © Linda Svendsen; design: Precision Cabinet & Trim; bottom left: © Mark Lohman; bottom right: © Carolyn Bates/www.carolynbates.com, design: Allen Koster

p. 227: Left: © Brian Vanden Brink; design; Morningstar Marble & Granite; top right: © Grey Crawford; bottom right: © Grey Crawford

INDEX